The Christmas Mystery

The Christmas Mystery

What on earth happened at Bethlehem?

Charles Foster

Authentic

MILTON KEYNES • COLORADO SPRINGS • HYDERABAD

Copyright © 2007 Charles Foster

13 12 11 10 09 08 07   7 6 5 4 3 2 1

First published 2007 by Authentic Media
9 Holdom Avenue, Bletchley, Milton Keynes, Bucks, MK1 1QR, UK
1820 Jet Stream Drive, Colorado Springs, CO 80921, USA
OM Authentic Media
Medchal Road, Jeedimetla Village, Secunderabad 500 055, A.P., India

www.authenticmedia.co.uk

Authentic Media is a division of IBS-STL UK, limited by guarantee, with
its Registered Office at Kingstown Broadway, Carlisle, Cumbria CA3 0HA.
Registered in England and Wales No. 1216232. Registered charity 270162.

The right of Charles Foster to be identified as the author of this work
has been asserted by him in accordance with the Copyright, Designs
and Patents Act 1988.

British Library Cataloguing in Publication Data
A catalogue record for this book is available from the British Library

ISBN 978–1–85078–769–3

The Scripture quotations contained herein are from the New Revised Standard
Version Bible, copyright © 1989, by the Division of Christian Education of the
National Council of the Churches of Christ in the USA, and are used
by permission. All rights reserved.

I am grateful to Regent College Press, Vancouver, for permission to use the
Charles Williams quotation at p. v, and to Richard Carrier for permission to use
his translations of the *Lapis Tiburtinus* (p. 37) and the *Lapis Venetus* (p. 42).
Unless otherwise stated, all illustrations are © Charles Foster.

Cover design by fourninezero design.
Typeset by Waverley Typesetters, Fakenham
Print Management by Adare
Printed in Great Britain by J.H. Haynes & Co., Sparkford

The beginning of Christendom is, strictly, at a point out of time. A metaphysical trigonometry finds it among the spiritual Secrets, at the meeting of two heavenward lines, one drawn from Bethany along the Ascent of Messias, the other from Jerusalem against the Descent of the Paraclete. That measurement, the measurement of the eternity in operation, of the bright cloud and the rushing wind is, in effect, theology.

The history of Christendom is the history of an operation ... Historically, its beginning was clear enough. There had appeared in Palestine, during the government of the Princeps Augustus and his successor Tiberius, a certain being. This being was in the form of a man ...

Charles Williams, The Descent of the Dove

To Lizzie and Sally:
I honestly thought that you were objectively the best
in the nativity play.

Contents

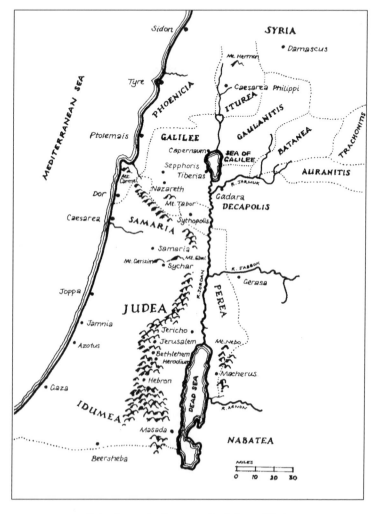

Palestine under Roman rule. © James Wade

Acknowledgements

Every book is a cocktail of the ideas of thousands of people. I have worried over these issues for years, and am grateful to all those who humoured me and helped to shape my thoughts.

It is invidious to name individuals, but I have to mention:

- Nicky Gumbel and Mike Lloyd of Holy Trinity Brompton, both of whom have an astonishing ability to keep their eyes on the theological ball when the play gets wild.
- James Wade, who gently and graciously put me right on the Greek and drew the splendid map at p. viii.
- Peter Crooks, formerly Canon of St George's Cathedral, Jerusalem, and now at Christ Church, Aden, who set me stumbling along the road to Bethlehem a long time ago.
- Richard Carrier, one of the most articulate atheists of his generation, whose passionate devotion to the truth has been an inspiration.
- My wife Mary, who dealt kindly and patiently with my absences. I'm sorry that such kindness and patience are so often necessary.

The errors and the bumptious opinions are of course entirely my own.

Preface

The church, by and large, does not celebrate Christmas. Of course many millions of people pack the churches at Christmastide, but the Biblical Christmas is almost never mentioned. The Catholics and the High Anglicans give thoughtful homilies on the wonder of the Incarnation and the submission of Mary. The Baptists talk about Christmas as the start of our journey into faith. The evangelicals often by-pass Christmas altogether, suggesting that the whole thing is pointless without Easter, and so here is the Easter sermon you really need to hear but probably won't bother to come for. But rarely is there any exploration of the real Christmas story.

It is not surprising. As soon as you go seriously into those two nativity accounts of Matthew and Luke there are some horrendous difficulties. They force evangelicals to examine just what they mean when they say that scripture is true. They force Catholics to wonder if they've read Mary right. They force historians to ask painful questions about the adequacy of their methods. They force everyone to ask if God really did germinate inside the womb of a Jewish girl.

I have dodged these accounts for years. But eventually I couldn't help looking. I had expected problems, but I hadn't begun to expect the compelling strangeness that I found there.

CHARLES FOSTER
London, May 2007

Chapter 1

Away in a manger

Last year, as every year, I went rather wearily to the school nativity play. And last year, as every year, the same story was told. An angel in a white sheet told a curiously unsurprised Mary that she was going to have a baby. Joseph, grey-bearded and leaning on a stick to indicate his advanced age, was slightly upset but was quickly reassured that his wife was still a nice Jewish girl. Mary and Elizabeth had some vaguely theological conversations during Mary's pregnancy, and then, when the holy couple had to head south from Nazareth because of the census, Mary was duly loaded onto a donkey. On arrival at Bethlehem, exhausted and with Mary already having some histrionic twinges, they found that there was no room at the inn. The innkeeper, though, was a kindly man, and he let them occupy the stable. And there, although the audience was spared the medical details, the baby Jesus was born. The children playing the ox, the ass and the sheep bent adoringly in papier-mâché masks over the doll in the manger, while hordes of tone-deaf angels serenaded the newborn king of the Jews. Shepherds came to the manger. In a new and hugely popular touch, the lambs they carried kissed the baby.

Then there was some vaguely oriental music, borrowed from the local tandoori restaurant, and in came the three kings on supposedly comic camels, pointing ostentatiously to a huge star dangling from a long cane. Mary proudly displayed the child to them, and was ecstatically grateful at the rich gifts of gold, frankincense and myrrh. The curtain fell with all the company assembled round the manger, singing 'Away in a manger'. Mary beamed beatifically as befitted a girl who had viciously seen off all her rivals for the role.

Afterwards, as we ate our mince pies and told our respective children that they were easily the best in the show, there were the inevitable attempts at jokes.

'I was really disappointed', said one father, on his third glass of cooking sherry. 'I was looking forward to the massacre of the innocents, and they missed it out.'

'Of course they did', rejoined another. 'They couldn't find any innocents in this school to massacre.'

A genuinely kind and godly woman, whom I know to be a pillar of her local church, came up to me and touched my arm. She knows that I write Christian books, and obviously felt I should be protected from all this.

'Don't you listen to them', she said. 'It's wonderful, isn't it, to be reminded of that great story?'

'It is', I said. 'It really is.' But all the time I was thinking: Which story is she talking about?

Two accounts: one story?

There are two accounts of the nativity in the canonical gospels. They are in Matthew and in Luke. It is not easy to read them together. On the face of it they look like completely different stories. In each of them, sure, Mary and Joseph are betrothed, and in Bethlehem Mary bears a son of unusual origin. But that's where the similarities end. Their family trees of Jesus are as different as a Christmas tree and a festive holly bush. In Matthew, Mary and Joseph appear to be residents of Bethlehem. There's no pre-birth travel involved, and indeed the elaborate story of Archelaus' rule over Judaea is later told to explain why the couple went to Nazareth. In Luke, Nazareth is the family home: he needs the problematic vehicle of Quirinius' census to bring them to Bethlehem. There's no inn in Matthew: Jesus is born conventionally in the house. And it is in the house that the magi, unknown to Luke, welcome him. For the other traditional visitors you have to go to Luke. There you will find the angel choirs and the shepherds abiding in the fields by night. Although Luke gives them a harrowing pre-natal journey, Mary and Joseph have a much quieter time in Luke than in Matthew. They bring Jesus to the Jerusalem temple in the prescribed way, Simeon and Anna predict great things for him, and then the family goes peaceably back home to Galilee.

Matthew is much darker: Herod, terrified that he might be usurped by Jesus, tries to recruit the wise men as his spies. When this plot fails, he kills all the children in the Bethlehem area who are two years old or younger. But the holy family, warned in a dream, have already fled to Egypt, where they stay until after the death of Herod. The original plan was evidently to return to Judaea, but since Herod's son Archelaus was ruling there, there's a change of plan. They divert to Nazareth.

You will search the Bible in vain for many of the other beloved details of the Christmas story. It is brutal to say it, but so far as we know from the gospels Jesus remained callously unadored by the oxen and asses.[1] There were no royal visitors – no kings:[2] just a group of eastern astrologers whose beliefs would attract the loudest tut-tuts from modern evangelicals. And we have no idea how many there were: it's only said that there were three because three types of gift were brought.

So there are problems. It cannot be denied. Deny it and you're plainly not reading things properly. And unless you realize that there's a problem, there's no chance at all of reaching a solution.

I wrote this book in the British Library in London's Euston Road. Just downstairs from the room where I worked there was a magnificent exhibition entitled *Sacred*. It was a look at some of the cornerstone texts of the three Abrahamic faiths. I went there often when I could take no more of Matthew, Luke or their detractors.

One of the most prized exhibits was a sixth-century CE commentary on the Diatessaron. The Diatessaron was a bold attempt by the second-century Assyrian Christian Tatian to harmonize the New Testament gospels. It doesn't exist anymore, and is known only by commentaries on it. It was strenuously suppressed by the early church. But why? Wasn't it a godly enterprise to show that the various gospel accounts hung effortlessly together? Well, the early church thought not. And they weren't stupid. They could see that Matthew and Luke didn't agree on the nativity story, and that the resurrection stories of the gospel writers were importantly different. They were engaged in apologetics just as modern Christians are. Yet they decided not only that they should live with the difficulties, but that the difficult versions were the only versions that the Church should have. They preferred authenticity to ease. They believed in truth, and believed that scripture contained it. They believed far more completely in the authority and the truthful witness of scripture than many so-called 'Bible-believing Christians' today. Would the modern Evangelical Church have resisted the temptation to edit the gospels into harmony? I hope so, but I sometimes doubt it. If the temptation is resisted, the apologist has a hard task, but not an impossible one. If you take these accounts seriously – if you read them with open eyes – they end up being hugely more convincing that the harmonized, sanitized, emasculated version of the fundamentalist imagination.

Why bother with this inquiry?

Every day Christians across the world stand and say loudly that they believe in Jesus Christ 'who was conceived by the Holy Spirit [and] born of the Virgin Mary ...' This is part of the Apostles' Creed, a statement of the lowest common denominators of the faith. Many think that if you can say the Creed, you're a Christian, and if you can't, you're not. Whether that's right or not, belief in the nativity story or stories is regarded as foundational. But is it?

The only mention of the birth of Jesus is in the nativity accounts of Matthew and Luke. Both Matthew and Luke of course base much of their respective gospels on Mark, which is almost universally agreed to have been the first gospel to be written down. But neither Mark nor John touches very obviously on the circumstances of Jesus' birth, even when you might expect them to. In John's Gospel Philip says to Nathanael: '"We have found him about whom Moses in the law and also the prophets wrote, Jesus son of Joseph from Nazareth". Nathanael said to him, "Can anything good come out of Nazareth?"'[3] This seems like an obvious cue for the comment: 'Well, as a matter of fact Jesus doesn't come from Nazareth at all. Nor is he really the son of Joseph.' But it never comes. That suggests to many that none of John's sources knew the Bethlehem or the virgin birth traditions, or if they did, they didn't believe them.[4] Yet John's gospel proceeds perfectly happily without the virgin birth[5]. None of the majestic theology of John would be any more secure if it rested on a well-attested miraculous birth at Bethlehem.

Some see Mark 6:3 as implicitly accepting the virgin birth: 'Is not this the carpenter?' asks the crowd there. 'The son of Mary and brother of James and Joses and Judas and Simon ... ' But that's really scraping the bottom of the apologetic barrel. The most we can sensibly say is that Mark doesn't contradict the virgin birth.

None of the New Testament letters hints at the idea of a virgin birth.[6] Christian apologists, desperate to find a miraculous conception in Paul, have sought to say that Galatians 4:4 implies a virgin birth: 'God sent his Son, born of a woman ... ' says the verse. Well, I was born of a woman too, but my father would take grave offence at the idea that he had nothing to do with it. The idiom 'born of a woman' was and remained at least until Elizabethan times a perfectly ordinary euphemism for normal biological arrival.

So: if the nativity story didn't matter to most of the New Testament, does it matter to us? Would it really matter if the nativity accounts were excised? Would our faith be any different without them?

It is certainly true that the mainstream church from very early times believed in the virgin birth.[7] We return to the evidence about this later. But nonetheless it can be argued convincingly that the accounts didn't really begin to *matter* theologically until the late fourth and fifth centuries with the elaboration of the doctrine of original sin. The infection of original sin was transmitted by sex, according to Augustine and the other high priests of the doctrine: Jesus wasn't infected because his conception had been sexless. This notion of the mechanics of human corruption is increasingly unpopular today, but it has exerted colossal influence on Christian thought.[8] It will be argued in this book that the doctrines of the immaculate conception of Mary (as distinct from the doctrine of the virginal conception of Jesus) and the perpetual virginity of Mary were consequences of this wrong view of sex and sin, which is ultimately a Gnostic one.

Christian theology can get by perfectly well without the nativity accounts. Why, then, spend time and energy examining them?

There are three reasons:

- The first is that if they are true, they presumably contain some important information which increases our ability to relate to God. I believe this to be the case, but the way that it helps us is not the subject of this book.

- The second is that Matthew and Luke make many clear assertions about the birth of Jesus. If they are wrong, either the authority of scripture is diminished, or our understanding of what is meant by the authority of scripture has to change.

- The third is that it is extremely interesting.

If we're going to read these curious accounts, we need to know *how* to read them.

Chapter 2

How to read the nativity accounts

My friend Ben, who is also a barrister, came round to my room in chambers. He flung himself in the armchair in the corner of the room, sighed deeply, and said: '*It were better that my mother had not borne me.*'

'Why's that?', I asked.

'I've had a wretched day', he said. 'The Tube was down, and I waited in a tunnel outside Edgware Road for just long enough to miss my connection at Paddington. I finally got to Oxford an hour late, and the judge was fuming. When I got started he was interrupting all the time. He said my arguments were pitifully thin and obviously unsustainable. He chewed me up and spat me out. He didn't even ask my opponent to reply before dismissing my application with costs against my client.'

'Oh dear', I said, and gave him a cup of tea. And that was all he needed. Twenty minutes later he was bouncing as ebulliently and as irritatingly as he generally does, talking about England's hopeless performance in the Test match and planning his holiday in Burgundy.

Imagine that an academic two thousand years hence has a transcript of Ben's opening line: all that she knows about Ben was that he had sat down in my room citing that despairing line from Hamlet. What would she write?

She might well write that Ben was suicidal – in the profoundest depths of existential angst, with everything that makes life worth living stripped cruelly away. She might speculate that Ben had taken his own life then and there. If her PhD thesis was hung entirely on this surviving fragment, she would have to go a lot further. She might wonder if his discontent arose from disturbing visions of his father's ghost. If she looked more closely at the passage she might think that Ben was talking to a lover with whom he couldn't quite get on, or was impliedly confessing that he was 'an arrant knave', and so perhaps facing prosecution for a criminal offence or (if she knew he was a barrister) discipline by the Bar Council.

In fact all her conclusions would be absurdly wrong. Her PhD would be worthless.

Now imagine that as well as the line from Shakespeare she also had the text of the conversation about the Tube and the courtroom débâcle. She would bend over backwards to link them. She would conclude that in the early twenty-first century an unfavourable comment from a petulant judge meant psychological and professional devastation – perhaps particularly (for arcane reasons developed in the book and the lectures that would no doubt follow her thesis) if the advocate was from the Danish royal family. She might spend a chapter, or possibly a career, discussing the 'chewed and spat out' line, taking it as evidence of judicial violence, and possibly cannibalism. Again she would be wholly wrong. She would have wasted her professional life.

She wouldn't have made these mistakes if she'd known Ben; known that he'd read English and loves to quote; known that like many in his profession he habitually overstates things; known that he's a bit of a drama queen. One has to be careful how one reads things. In reading things right it helps to know who has written them. The best person to have told our academic about Ben would have been Ben himself. And if we're going to read Matthew and Luke, the best people to tell us how to read them are Matthew and Luke themselves.

Two accounts: helpful or problematic?

The differences between Matthew and Luke create problems: no doubt about it. But they also dispose of some problems. No one could ever, ever, accuse Matthew and Luke of getting their heads together. When they deal with the nativity story, no one could ever accuse them of being parasitic on Mark, as they are elsewhere in their gospels. Whatever we've got here, we have two plainly different sources making broadly the same point about the miraculous birth of Jesus.

Only two accounts: helpful or problematic?

We have noted already that Matthew and Luke are the only two gospel writers to mention the Christmas events, and that Christmas doesn't appear elsewhere in the New Testament. Does this constitute a real challenge to the historicity of the story?

Well, hardly. The gospels don't purport to be biographies of Jesus. Luke, with his expressed intention to write an 'orderly account' of the events of Jesus' life,[9] provides the nearest thing to a biography that we have. Yet even Luke has his agenda – to demonstrate how the life and death of Jesus are the consequence of a divine plan.[10] Luke's birth story fits very well with that overall agenda. Matthew, too, is keen to show by constant citation how the Hebrew scriptures prefigured almost everything about Jesus' life. It's not surprising that he starts that exercise at the very beginning.

Mark moves fast, vividly and artlessly towards the suffering and death of Jesus. It is not difficult to understand why he would have little interest in how things started.

John is very frank about his objective. He wanted to persuade his readers 'to believe that Jesus is the Messiah, the Son of God', and to 'have life in his name'.[11] If he knew of the nativity story, presumably he thought that it didn't help to advance that agenda. John's notion of Messiahship is rather different to Matthew's: continuity with David doesn't seem to matter much to him. He says expressly that there is plenty of other material that he could have used.[12] He has had to be selective. Perhaps the nativity story was left on the cutting room floor.

John, anyway, doesn't neglect Jesus' origins: he paints them on a grand, cosmic canvas: 'In the beginning was the Word ... '[13] For John, a detailed description of the mechanics of the enfleshment of the Word would detract from his epic.

As so often, the detail is so intoxicating that it is easy to lose sight of the big picture. The fact is that Jesus *was* born in *some* circumstances. Both John and Mark were perfectly capable of using whatever circumstances they were to make some points helpful to the case for Jesus that they were trying to mount. They chose not to do so. The fact that they chose not to do so doesn't mean that Jesus wasn't born. And similarly their silence about the miraculous events of Bethlehem doesn't begin to mean that those events didn't happen as Matthew and Luke say they did. Nor does it imply that the events of the birth were so shameful that they needed to be brushed under the carpet. If that were so, Matthew and Luke would have been much better advised to take the same line rather than to invite embarrassing contradiction by mentioning them when it wasn't theologically vital to do so. Although it is probably true that Matthew and Luke weren't written down until the second half of the first century, the stories that were ultimately committed to papyrus were obviously circulating in the churches of the eastern Mediterranean long before that, exposed to critics well placed to contradict inaccuracy, mendacity or plain myth-weaving.

The genealogies: Divine origins and literary agendas

I spend most of my life examining the accounts of witnesses and evaluating the differences between them. In evaluating X's evidence a useful, if rather obvious, preliminary question to ask is: 'Why is X saying what he is saying?' In the cases of both Matthew and Luke that is a good question too. And a surprisingly illuminating place to visit in the search for the answer is the genealogy section in each gospel.

Biblical genealogies are an acquired taste. Most people never acquire it, and I can see why. The names are long, unpronounceable and obscure. And there's also the feeling that they are irrelevant because we know the end of the story anyway: we know that Jesus was the anointed Messiah who had been foreseen by the prophets of Israel and who would die for the remission of sins. Why then burden us with all the tedious ancestral background?

There are many answers to that question, but here's one. They tell us something of what the writer's agenda is: what he's getting at. They help us to get onto the writer's wavelength: to read the rest of the story more intelligently. Matthew and Luke weren't quaint antiquarians who thought that the ancestry of Jesus ought to be written down simply because it was there. The genealogies weren't meant to sit in a glass cabinet being gazed at respectfully: they were meant to be *used*.

A word here: There's nothing heretical about saying that a gospel writer had an agenda. Christians don't (or shouldn't) read the Bible as Muslims read the Qu'ran – as words dictated from on high and merely inscribed onto parchment by a human secretary. Matthew and Luke were more than mere *styli*. The genesis of their versions is more complex, and so ultimately more historically convincing than that.

Many points need to be made about the two genealogies of Jesus in Matthew and Luke. They are forcefully made by all articulate opponents of Christianity.

The genealogies are different

They are radically different, too. From Adam to Abraham, Luke is on his own. From Abraham to David, Luke and Matthew agree. From David to Joseph they differ completely with the sole exceptions of Zerubabel and his father Salathiel. Matthew has forty-two generations between Jesus and Abraham, and only twenty-eight between Jesus and David. Luke has fifty-six between Jesus and Abraham, of which forty-two are between Jesus and David. From Zerubabel, Matthew comes to the end of the Old Testament record on which his genealogy has been based. Thereafter, both he and Luke depend on documents of which the Old Testament knows nothing, and which specifically contradict the Old Testament.[14]

There have been brave and hopeless attempts to reconcile Matthew and Luke. The third-century apologist Julius Africanus was the first one to step into the ring. The discrepancies are explained, he said, by the law of Leviratic marriage. If a man died leaving a childless widow, Jewish law required the dead man's brother to marry the widow. The first resulting male heir was regarded legally as the son of the deceased brother. There's the solution, said Julius:

one list is the list of biological fathers; the other is the list of legal fathers.

But it doesn't work. Just think how many dead brothers you'd need to square the circle. And what about all the generations in the shorter Matthew genealogy that are simply missing?

Others have suggested that the genealogies are different because they are genealogies of different people: Matthew gives Joseph's; Luke gives Mary's. But this is just as far-fetched.

There's not the slightest hint in Luke that he's tracing Mary's line, and indeed that would be a deeply eccentric thing to do. Luke says expressly: 'Jesus … was the son (as was thought) of Joseph, son of Heli, son of Matthat …',[15] and so on. Matthew ends his list by saying: '… Jacob the father of Joseph the husband of Mary, of whom Jesus was born …'[16] But suppose one of these verses is untrue, and one of the genealogies really is the genealogy of Mary. What about the numbers of generations? It would mean that the side of the family described by Matthew was hugely longer-lived than that in Luke's account. And yet from Abraham to David Mary and Joseph share entirely common ancestors.

Try as hard and as imaginatively as you like; reconciliation is impossible.[17] It's not the proper job of Christian apologetics to harmonize where it can't be done. It makes the faith look ridiculous. We have to learn to live with the fact that scripture doesn't, on its surface, tell a completely consistent story.

This is a liberating and enlightening revelation. In the very first chapter of the very first book of the New Testament we hear, loud and clear, the death knell of scriptural literalism. But that same noise announces the birth of another doctrine that can't be so easily dismissed. There's no name for that doctrine, but it's the notion that the deeper you dig into these extraordinary books, the more durable the truths that can be mined. We underestimate the complexity of scripture at our peril. Scripture, like people, is multi-layered, and coruscates with nuance. I wouldn't be respecting my friends, and I certainly wouldn't understand a word they were saying, if I took them literally. Remember Ben. Should it be any different with these books? As we peel away our presumptions about the way that scripture is to be read, we begin to see other things beneath. This is a million miles from flaccid, anaemic liberalism, and is based on a much higher view of scripture than literalism. It's no accident that literalism, which makes scripture literally unbelievable, is rubbished in the opening lines of the story of Jesus. A.N. Wilson, in his biography *Jesus*, has a very stimulating chapter entitled 'How to read a Gospel'. Matthew, by confronting us with some barn-door difficulties that we're bound to see, gives us an even more stimulating and much more useful lesson in how to do exactly that.

How did the discrepancies between the genealogies arise? I don't know, and nor does anyone else. It is speculated that Matthew and Luke had different lists of Davidic ancestors: several were no doubt in circulation at the time. The suggestion that Herod the Great, worried about his own dismally un-Davidic credentials, suppressed all genealogies, leaving everyone groping in the dark, is unconvincing. The attempted suppression is unlikely to have been very effective. More interesting is the observation that the New Testament genealogies don't even agree with the Old Testament. All that Matthew and Luke had to do to get those bits right was to ask the local rabbi if they could check something in the Torah scroll. They knew, too, that they could easily have been checked up on themselves. So they're either being very slapdash, or absolute historical accuracy isn't the point.

But what *is* the point? It is to tell us something about Jesus. What that is is something that emerges after we have looked at some of the other objections.

Are they genealogies of Jesus at all?

They're not if you believe that Joseph was not the biological father of Jesus. They both seem to be genealogies of Joseph, as would be the norm for Jewish genealogies. Some commentators think that Luke's genealogy was originally asserting that Joseph *was* Jesus' father, and that in the line 'Jesus ... was the son (as was thought) of Joseph'[18] the words 'as was thought' were a late scribal addition.[19] There is no textual evidence for this at all: it is one of many depressing examples of people assuming scribal dishonesty whenever the Biblical record doesn't fit with their theses.[20]

The purpose of both genealogies seems to be to link Jesus to the Davidic line. And the purpose of doing this is to establish his Messianic credentials. Both Matthew and Luke have Jesus born in Bethlehem, the city of David, and Matthew, as we will see, uses and appears to abuse the Old Testament in order to bolster the Messianic case. But in the genealogies themselves, neither Matthew nor Luke plead the Davidic claim in the most obvious way. Luke lists David as only one of many forebears, and, unlike Matthew, traces the Davidic line not through the illustrious blood of Solomon and the kings of Judah but down a really obscure little genetic alley – through Nathan – a son of David whose legendarily obscure descendants never made it either to the throne or into the Hebrew Bible.

Why? Again we can only speculate. But perhaps Luke was saying that this Messiah is different: he will flout your expectations: he's coming in from a side that will surprise you. Don't expect a military hero like David. But if we're interested in historicity, note this. Both Luke and Matthew regard Jewish history as the servant of the Messiah: they use it to illuminate him. Does that mean that the basic story they're telling isn't true? Absolutely not.

Matthew stakes the Messianic claim in a heady mix of the blindingly obvious and the eye-crossingly cryptic. Matthew, as we've seen, wields the editorial blue pencil savagely. He has fewer people in the list, but the ones who are there are big: David, Solomon, Rehoboam, Uzziah and so on. He seems to cut out everyone who is not a charismatic royal celebrity. Jesus is the royal Messiah, he's saying: just look at the blood in those veins.

Then comes the strangeness, in an initially unpromising form: 'So all the generations from Abraham to David are fourteen generations; and from David to the deportation to Babylon, fourteen generations; and from the deportation to Babylon to the Messiah, fourteen generations.'[21] I have yawned my way through this verse for years. But I'm the poorer for it. If I'd have thought about it I would have realized two extraordinarily odd things about the verse.

The first is that it is the result of some very careful editorial massaging by the author. As we've noted, Matthew gives Jesus many fewer ancestors than does Luke. So why does he massage the list into these three groups of fourteen? Theories abound, but the most popular and the most reputable is that the name 'David' is itself the key. Hebrew *gematria* assigns numerical values to letters. David's name has three consonants, the numerical value of which amounts to fourteen:

$$d + w + d = 4 + 6 + 4 = 14.$$

You could hardly have a more fundamental assertion of Davidic Messianic royalty than this. 'David, David, David' screams at you from the unseen depths of the passage.

The second is even odder. I've got three groups of fourteen, says Matthew. But in fact he hasn't. The last group is missing one: there are only thirteen generations in the last run up to Jesus.

This has brought the cryptographers out in force. There are a few obvious things to note about it. The first is that Matthew wasn't stupid. He could count. That suggests that he meant something by it. The second is that the later editors of the New Testament weren't stupid either. They could count too. It is, like so many things in the nativity stories, impressive testimony to the integrity of those early editors that they didn't add a generation in a misguided attempt to spare Matthew's blushes. So they thought either that Matthew meant something by it, or that if it was a slip, it was a slip that the Holy Spirit had rubber-stamped.

If Matthew meant something by it, what might that be? We can only ever guess, but the most theologically coherent guess is that the missing fourteenth generation was the risen, transformed Jesus. Matthew is hinting that there's a brand new kingdom on the way, somehow in the line of David, but not sufficiently in the line of David to be listed there.[22]

This is all very well, but it doesn't take us very far in answering the question of why the genealogies of Joseph are there at all. We've established that the genealogies are there to link Jesus to David, but they can only do that if Joseph is the biological father of Jesus, which both gospels, at least at this stage, seem to be insistent that he's not. So surely they either fail in their purpose of establishing the Davidic link, or fail in their purpose of establishing virgin birth?

Without abandoning the virgin birth, which the text seems to me to forbid, there is no obvious way out of this conundrum. But remember what we've already noted.

Whatever you say about them, Matthew and Luke are no fools. They are able redactors, and capable of writing complex, sophisticated, allusive and elusive books. It simply cannot be the case that they failed to note the difficulty they had created. The same goes for later editors. It would have been the work of moments to eliminate with a few strokes of a deceitful stylus the whole apparent inconsistency. But it was never done. There is a dismal inconsistency in many liberal commentaries on the nativity stories. They are prepared to credit Matthew and Luke with a remarkable capacity for literary elaboration, but with no ability at all to see an anomaly that an average eight year old would spot at once.

Matthew and Luke must have meant to convey something by this. Probably it was something along these lines: Jesus' Jewish, and indeed Davidic, credentials are unimpeachable. We challenge anyone to dispute it. The connection with David is through the Jewish law of filiation. If, then, you say that Jesus was the fruit of Joseph's loins, he's still got all the qualifications that any Messiah could look for. And even if you don't think that he was Joseph's natural son, the law makes him just as much David's heir as if he were. So whether you're whispering about illegitimacy, or doubting the virgin birth, be quiet: however you play it, this is the Messiah. But he's a strange Messiah. Although he ticks all the prophetic boxes, he is not what was expected. Even the prophets who wrote about him didn't see properly what they were writing about. Down an unlooked-for by-way of Jewish history comes a Messiah to shatter scripture's preconceptions, and yours.

The problem of Matthew's women

Matthew's genealogy has at least one other level of code embedded in it. This time the coded bits are easy to spot, although the decoding is not easy at all. Matthew mentions four women (apart from Mary herself). They are Tamar, Rahab, Bathsheba and Ruth. This would have jumped out at any first century reader as very odd indeed.

If it was odd to mention women at all, it was particularly odd to mention these women. There are two obvious things linking them. First: all the women have a foreign husband or are of foreign origin themselves. Tamar was probably a Canaanite, and Rahab certainly was. Bathsheba was the wife of Uriah the Hittite, and Ruth was from Moab. And second: all but Ruth have a murky sexual past. Tamar, posing as a prostitute, seduced her father-in-law.[23] Rahab was a harlot in Jericho.[24] The sight of Bathsheba bathing inflamed David to adultery and murder.[25] It is even suggested that Ruth led Boaz on in an unseemly way, but the case against her is not so obvious.[26]

Non-Jewishness and sex: what was Matthew thinking of? In citing the role of non-Jews in producing the Messiah, perhaps he was seeking to broaden Jesus' appeal to non-Jews, saying that they too could come into the Messianic fold. Or perhaps he was implicitly dealing with some criticisms of Jesus' own credentials. We don't know much about Mary, but perhaps she was not of impeccable Jewish stock. If so, Matthew might have been demonstrating that this was no obstacle to true Jewish Kingship: David's own past hardly bore close inspection. Or perhaps the mentions are markers of some arcane internecine debate about the nature of the Messiah. The high priestly Sadducees were very keen on pure Jewish blood, and would have been slow to accept a Messiah with eugenic blemishes. Matthew's response is a pretty typical (and devastating) Pharisaical rejoinder.

The sexual references, too, are probably a response to questions about Jesus' origins. Some see in Mark 6:3 an innuendo about Jesus' illegitimacy: 'Is not this the carpenter, the son of Mary?' the crowd says. If there's an innuendo, it is: 'He's got no father.' The verse was certainly taken that way in antiquity.[27] It wouldn't be surprising if there were such rumours. Indeed the existence of such rumours is some indication that the non-biological paternity of Jesus was being asserted during his lifetime or very shortly afterwards.

We know that stories about Jesus' illegitimacy were being peddled around quite early. Origen rages against the calumnies spread in about 178 CE by the pagan writer Celsus.[28] Mary had an affair with a soldier called Panthera, said Celsus. Mary's husband, a carpenter, found out, and divorced her, and she had to eke out a living by spinning.[29] Tertullian relates late second century Jewish rumours of Mary being a prostitute, and the fourth-century apocryphal book *The Acts of Pilate*, whose sources might go back to the second century, records that Jews were saying that Jesus was the fruit of an adulterous liaison. These rumours were elaborated and embodied in the Talmud. Miriam, the mother of Jesus, was a hair-dresser, according to several of the rabbis.[30] She was married to a man called Stada, but she also had a lover, Pandera, who fathered Jesus.

If this is any indication of the sort of mutterings on the first century Palestinian streets (and it probably is), it is not surprising that Matthew enlists those fallen Old Testament heroines. He only enlists them to support a fall-back position, of course. His primary case is plainly that Jesus was born to a virgin. It is worth stating this, because his desire to say that irregular ancestry doesn't disqualify Jesus from Messiahship has been seized on by some to say that he doesn't really believe in the virgin birth. He very obviously does – of which more later. But he does a belt-and-braces job, saying that if, which is denied, Jesus was the result of an extra-marital liaison, so what? Look at how the Jewish world has been blessed in the past by the offspring from such unions.

The genealogies: a summary

We tend to skip the genealogies, but that is very dangerous. They give us some clear and salutary lessons in how they and the other parts of the nativity accounts are to be read. History plainly matters to the writers: it is important to them that Jesus is located in Jewish history. But they expound history at the same time as telling it. The result is a literary medium that we're not used to. To characterize it as unhistorical is to miss the point completely. To characterize it as pure history that in some unknown way can be reconciled without violence to everything else we know of Biblical history is to miss the point just as badly.

Matthew's curious use of the Old Testament

Matthew plays fast and loose with the Old Testament. He consistently misquotes. In any reputable orthodox seminary he would get an outright fail in his Old Testament papers.

Isaiah 7:14

This is the famous passage that Matthew[31] and Handel[32] so resonantly render as 'Behold, a virgin shall conceive and bear a son: and shall call his name Emmanuel ...' The difficulty is well known. We deal with it in detail in a later chapter, but it forms part of the indictment against Matthew at this stage. He follows the translators of the Septuagint (the most important Greek translation of the Old Testament, probably complete by 132 BCE) in translating the Hebrew word *almah,* (which is more conventionally translated as 'young woman'), as *parthenos* – virgin.

The first thing to note about this and about all the other Old Testament misquotes in Matthew, is that it cannot be a mere mistake. If Luke had written Matthew's gospel the case for a mistake would be much stronger. Luke was a gentile, and wasn't marinated in Jewish culture as thoroughly as the other gospel writers. But everybody agrees that Matthew was a Jew, and a very Jewish Jew at that. He was brought up having the Hebrew Bible read to him every week. He knew perfectly well that the Hebrew text of Isaiah said *almah*. For whatever reason he deliberately opted for the Septuagint version – a version more alien to him than the Hebrew one.

Micah 5:2
Micah says:

> But you, O Bethlehem of Ephrathah, who are one of the little clans of Judah, from you shall come forth for me one who is to rule in Israel, whose origin is from of old, from ancient days.

Matthew, though, says something rather different. He is quoting from a Greek translation again, but this time not the Septuagint. He says that the chief priests and scribes of the people told Herod that the Messiah would be born:

> In Bethlehem of Judea; for so it has been written by the prophet: 'And you, Bethlehem, in the land of Judah, are by no means least among the rulers of Judah; for from you shall come a ruler who is to shepherd my people Israel.'[33]

Note what has happened. The Old Testament belittles Bethlehem: it is a tiny, obscure place. But Matthew quotes Micah as saying precisely the opposite: Bethlehem is 'by no means the least' because the Messiah comes from there. The verb 'shepherd' is added, presumably to ring Davidic bells with his audience. This time he can't blame the Septuagint: he can't even say that his version is a gloss on the Septuagint. The Septuagint preserves all the sense of the Hebrew original.

Matthew seems to have a relaxed relationship with the Old Testament.

Hosea 11:1

Matthew, dealing with Herod's plot to murder Jesus, tells us that Joseph took Mary and Jesus to Egypt, where they remained until the death of Herod. 'This', he says, 'was to fulfil what had been spoken by the Lord through the prophet, "Out of Egypt I have called my son."'[34]

Is this really what the prophet said? The prophet in question is Hosea, and this time Matthew's quotation is nearly right. There is one enlightening 'mistake'. Hosea uses 'sons', plural. This is not reproduced in the New RSV, but is clear in the original. The entire verse, appropriately pluralized, reads: 'When Israel was a child, I loved him, and out of Egypt I called my sons.' The English translation of the following verse confirms the original sense: 'The more I called them, the more they went from me; they kept sacrificing to the Baals, and offering incense to idols.'[35]

Hosea is plainly talking about the people of Israel. This is not a passage about the Messiah at all. To paraphrase *The Life of Brian*: the Messiah would indeed have been a very naughty boy if he had sacrificed to the Baals and offered incense to idols.

The obscure reference to 'Nazorean'

This is very strange. After Herod's death, the holy family return to Israel from Egypt. The details of their intentions are significant in another context which we come to later, but the upshot is that they go to Nazareth. This is another fulfilment of prophecy, according to Matthew. It is 'so that what had been spoken through the prophets might be fulfilled: "He will be called a Nazorean." '[36] The problem is that we have no idea which prophets Matthew purports to quote from. They are not (or at least not obviously) in the canonical Old Testament or the Apocrypha.

The imagination of the commentators, unfettered by any real information, has run wild over the meaning of 'the Nazorean'. Perhaps it came from some prophetic book, now lost. If it did, then whatever else the reference tells us about Matthew's Bible-reading habits, it is clear that he didn't think that the only kosher prophets were those between the covers of the canonical Hebrew Bible.

This would be an uncomfortable conclusion for many, and so many have strained to find the reference in the Old Testament. It's not easily done. Some think that we've got here a word play on *netzer* (branch), in Isaiah 11:1: 'A shoot shall come out from the stump of Jesse, and a branch shall grow out of his roots',[37] making this yet another assertion that Jesus is from the Davidic line. The best response to that is: 'Hmm': the Davidic point has been made in far more convincing ways elsewhere, and this, after all, is a passage about why Jesus is in Galilee and why he is *not* in the Davidic town of Bethlehem. Others think that it indicates that Jesus was a Nazirite. The Nazirites were a consecrated order who didn't cut their hair and who abstained from alcohol.[38] I think the case for a teetotal Jesus is as utterly unarguable as the case for a moon made of cream cheese, but there's a massive industry that disagrees with me. It notes, for example, that the crucified Jesus, having tasted wine on the sponge, refused to drink it,[39] but surely such a construction is wholly overwhelmed by Jesus' reputation as a 'drunkard',[40] his willingness to turn water into wine to liven up the party at Cana,[41] and the whole institution of the Eucharist?[42]

Making Jesus a Nazirite is at odds with everything we know about his life, and the Nazirites of old don't really prefigure Jesus at all. The most famous is of course Samson, who stalked around smiting with a donkey's jawbone and finally brought the Philistines' temple down upon himself and them.[43] You *can* see parallels between Samson and Jesus if you try hard enough. You can see parallels between any two things in the universe if you try hard enough. But it really won't do.

So what are we left with after looking at Matthew's Nazorean reference? We're left with bafflement. We simply don't know what he was getting at. And that itself is a useful conclusion. The world really doesn't end if we read a bit of the Bible and say: 'I haven't the first idea what this is about.' In fact some valuable things can begin with that bafflement.

Putting it together: Matthew and the Old Testament

Matthew has misquoted entirely deliberately from some major Old Testament sources. What's more, he has misquoted in a way which would have been blatantly obvious to his Jewish readers. There is no question of Matthew trying to deceive his readers into thinking that his quotations were the real text of the Hebrew scriptures, fulfilled in Jesus. The only possible conclusion is that he thought that the Hebrew scriptures he cites weren't completely right: they saw through a glass darkly. But the gospel writer's source has seen Jesus face to face. He knows what the prophets more or less dimly foresaw. And so (as we saw in the genealogies) he feels an obligation to *expound* those old texts as he goes along. The Hebrew scriptures are the true servant of the Messiah and so can be rewritten in the light of what is now clear about him. Yes, the Hebrew scriptures were indeed divinely inspired: but the clarity of the inspiration is hugely greater now that Jesus has landed. This is not being cavalier about scripture: far from it. It is reading scripture in the light of everything that is known about it; and that's a good canon of construction.

Matthew's intense respect for the Hebrew scriptures is shown well by the most difficult of the passages: Hosea 11:1. There are no two ways about it: in handling Hosea he has plainly ripped a verse brutally out of the context in which it appears to have been written, and then changed a divinely inspired plural to a singular. No modern expositor would dream of doing such a thing, and quite rightly. Why did Matthew bother? The point of the story, plainly, is to say that Jesus is the new Moses, ready to lead his people out of spiritual bondage. But it wasn't necessary to indulge in exegetical subterfuge to make that point: it would have been made perfectly adequately simply by saying that the holy family went to Egypt and then came back. No remotely literate Jew would have failed to get the right end of the expository stick. If some sort of Old Testament endorsement were needed, any attentive Sunday school child could think of an apparently more apposite verse. But Matthew opts to twist and rip. Why? Because he thinks that scripture is immensely complex, laminated, resonant and deep. He sees connections where we don't. The key to reading Matthew is to know that he has a much higher view of scripture than we do.

Matthew's handling of the Old Testament isn't a licence for the sort of literary clairvoyance we often see. There are few things more depressing and tedious than the sight of a preacher hunched over a metaphorical ouija board, telling us that he's been mysteriously led to read something between the lines of scripture that plainly isn't there. Matthew had a number of advantages over us.

Moving on

We've seen that it's a mistake to underestimate the subtlety of these accounts. We've seen that their writers (and particularly Matthew), were steeped in the Hebrew scriptures and saw nuances in them that we would never guess at. We've seen that Matthew is happy to say about prophetic passages: 'Yes, but I know the full story, and what the prophet was really trying to say was ... ' We've seen that it is not always easy to identify the 'merely' historical parts of them, and that a narrow literalism is hopeless. Very importantly, though, it is plain that Matthew and Luke are telling a story that they believe is historically true, and each got his version of the story from a different source. We need to be careful not to throw out the historical baby with the expository bathwater. Yes, Matthew spends a lot of time telling us why things happened. Sometimes those reasons are obscure. But does that mean that they didn't happen? Of course not. Many of the liberal critics of the nativity stories miss this. Matthew is only bothering to expound the nativity events by reference to the Hebrew scriptures *because* he is clear that those events actually happened. The point needs to be laboured: if they hadn't happened, he wouldn't ever have turned to Isaiah, Hosea and Micah to explain their significance.

Now that we've looked at how we should be reading Matthew and Luke, we need to come back to them to see exactly what they say and what they don't say. The first really important discrepancy between them relates to the date of Jesus' birth. And central to an exploration of the discrepancy is the issue of the census that Luke speaks about.

Chapter 3

The date and the census

A little while ago I wrote a book about the resurrection of Jesus. In the course of the research for that I spent a lot of time in Jerusalem. One evening I arranged to meet a well-known Christian archaeologist and apologist from one of the American Protestant churches. I'll call him John. He spends his life contending that the Christian contentions about Jesus are true. We sat in the Armenian tavern eating hummus and meatballs, and talking about his work. I had spent several days padding round first-century Jewish tombs, and had been struck again, as I always am when I'm in Jerusalem, by the vulnerability of the central Christian claims – a necessary consequence, it seems to me, of their historicity.

'So, John', I asked. 'What would make you lose your faith?'

'Nothing', he said, without hesitation. 'Nothing at all.'

'But what if the bones of Jesus were dug up tomorrow?'

He waved a hand dismissively. 'They couldn't possibly be. He rose from the dead on the Third Day.'

'But what if they were?'

'It couldn't happen.'

'But supposing it did. Suppose someone produced incontrovertible evidence that showed that the resurrection accounts were fairy tales. How would it affect you?'

He put his fork down wearily, and sighed. 'It wouldn't bother me in the slightest. There can be no such evidence. If anyone produced it, it would be a Satanic counterfeit, and it would spur me on all the more to preach the gospel.'

'But if that's the case, then why bother to engage in apologetics at all?' I persisted. 'Surely if you couldn't possibly be dissuaded from the faith by any historical or other evidence, then you can't really think that the evidence for the faith matters much either. How can you expect people to take your evidence seriously if you're not really relying on that evidence yourself? That seems unfair. It seems, I'm afraid to say, rather dishonest.'

I had put this clumsily, and he was stung.

'Now listen', he said. 'The evidence for the faith is massive. Many people are persuaded by it. I see it as my job to collect it and present it. But ultimately the evidence is subservient to the eternal truths of the gospel. If there's a battle between the evidence and the gospel, then the gospel wins every time.'

'But can there ever be a real battle between the evidence and the gospel?', I asked, genuinely wanting to know. 'Can the God of the gospel – the God of truth – ever want us to believe something that appears contrary to the truth?'

'Very often, I should think', he said. 'Blessed are those who do not see, and yet believe, remember? And now I really have to go.'

It was just as well that he had to go, because I was getting very cross.

John's view of the relevance of evidence is a very common one. I think it's a profoundly regrettable one, and one that has done the case for Christianity immense harm. 'The cost of being dishonest about the evidence is far greater than the cost of acknowledging that the Bible does not always give accurate historical data', wrote one commentator.[44] As a statement about the efficacy of apologetic strategy this is unquestionably true. As a statement of personal morality and a statement of the way that God wants us to see scripture I think it is true too. Perhaps we never really have to choose between believing scripture and believing the evidence. But unless we're really honest about the evidence we'll never find out if there's an irreconcilable conflict at all. Put another way, we can't be thrillingly reassured unless we're prepared to hear the worst.

When it comes to the clash between the nativity story and the available historical and archaeological data, the business of the census is just about as bad as it gets.

The problem

Luke writes: 'In those days a decree went out from Emperor Augustus that all the world should be registered. This was the first registration and was taken while Quirinius was governor of Syria. All went to their own towns to be registered. Joseph also went from the town of Nazareth in Galilee to Judea, to the city of David, called Bethlehem, because he was descended from the house and family of David. He went to be registered with Mary, to whom he was engaged, and who was expecting a child ...'[45]

When was this? Well, according to the Jewish historian Josephus, Quirinius became legate of Syria after Archelaus, the son of Herod the Great, was deposed. Archelaus was deposed in 6 CE.

If you read just Luke and Josephus together, then, Jesus seems to have been born in or after 6 CE.

But we also have Matthew. Matthew is perfectly clear: Jesus was born during the time of 'King Herod'. According to Matthew, Herod killed all the children in Bethlehem who were two years old or under.[46] This might imply that the holy family lived in Bethlehem for up to two years after the birth of Jesus, or perhaps Herod was just erring on the safe side. At any rate, it is not until Herod dies, and his son Archelaus ruled over Judea in his place,[47] that Joseph, Mary and Jesus return from their exile in Egypt and head to Galilee. Herod died in or around 4 BCE.

So there's the problem: Matthew seems to say that Jesus was born prior to 4 BCE: Luke seems to say that he was born after 6 CE.[48]

Various solutions have been attempted.[49] They all assume that the death of Herod is accurately dated to 4 BCE or thereabouts, and indeed the evidence for this is overwhelming.[50] The attempted solutions accordingly try to push Luke's date for the census and the birth back, rather than push Matthew's date forwards.

Nazareth, where the Annunciation is said to have occurred.
The prominent central building is the Church of the Annunciation.
© www.HolylandPhotos.org

The general secular consensus is that the discrepancies are irreconcilable. Richard Carrier summarizes it
well: 'There is no way to rescue the Gospels of Matthew
and Luke from contradicting one another ... The
contradiction is plain and irrefutable, and stands as
proof of the fallibility of the Bible, as well as the
falsehood of at least one of the two New Testament
accounts of the birth of Jesus.'[51] That consensus has
been massively boosted by the way that some Christian
apologists have handled the issue. There is nothing more
comforting for an advocate than to see his opponent
squirm and twist to get off the hook. Juries don't take
long to come to a conclusion where someone's doing
that.

Does Luke give us any other clues?

Yes he does. He says that 'in the days of King Herod of
Judea'[52] the angel Gabriel told Zechariah that his wife
Elizabeth would conceive. She duly did, although it is not
quite clear when she did so. The text says simply that 'after
those days his wife Elizabeth conceived ...'[53] The clear
implication, though, is that the conception (which was of
John the Baptist), happened 'in the days of King Herod of
Judea'. One apparently little point, which turns out to be
a big one, is that the word that Luke uses here for 'king'
is '*basileos*' (see below).

It was in the sixth month of Elizabeth's pregnancy that
the annunciation to Mary occurred, according to Luke.[54]
Again, it is not spelled out, but the obvious sense of the
passage is that the conception of Jesus occurred at or
around the time of the annunciation. If that's right, then
assuming that both John and Jesus had a normal gestation
period, Jesus was just 6 months younger than John, and
both would seem to have been born in (or if he had died

in the interim), very shortly after the reign of 'King Herod of Judea'.

But who was 'King Herod of Judea' at the beginning of Luke? It is not clear. It might be Herod the Great's son, Archelaus.[55] Archelaus, no doubt wanting to bask in his father's reflected glory, called himself 'Herod': there are coins in the Israel Museum to prove it. Josephus, too, called Archelaus a 'king'.[56] If Luke is talking about Archelaus, we are still in the same difficulty as before.

But Luke doesn't stop there. He is exhaustingly precise about the time when John the Baptist began his ministry. It was '... in the fifteenth year of the reign of Emperor Tiberius, when Pontius Pilate was governor of Judea, and Herod was ruler of Galilee, and his brother Philip ruler of the region of Ituraea and Trachonitis, and Lysanias ruler of Abilene, during the high priesthood of Annas and Caiaphas ...'[57]

Note that Luke doesn't use the word '*basileos*' to describe this Herod. He uses the word 'tetrarch', which fits Archelaus much more neatly. Surely he is distinguishing him from the Herod in whose reign Jesus was born?

Luke gives us plenty of chronological cross-bearings here. There's no doubt about the date: it was 28 CE. Now jump a few verses down the same chapter. Luke tells us that when Jesus began his ministry he was 'about thirty years old'.[58] Again, it is not absolutely clear, but this seems to be talking about more or less the same time as John began his ministry. So if Luke thinks that Jesus was 'about thirty' in 28 CE, Luke could well be agreeing broadly with Matthew about Jesus' chronology. If that's right, then all we're still arguing about is whether Luke was right about the census, and the issue of the census becomes very much less important than it appeared at first.

The fallibility of Josephus

The case against Luke depends on a single uncorroborated witness: Josephus. Luke is only in trouble if:

(a) Josephus is correct in placing the advent of Quirinius as legate of Syria after the accession of Archelaus; *and*

(b) The Quirinius that Luke is speaking of can *only* be the Quirinius that Josephus is speaking of.

Josephus is a great and important historian. But he is far from an infallible one. The *Encyclopaedia Britannica* says of him: 'As a historian, Josephus shares the faults of most ancient writers: his analyses are superficial, his chronology faulty, his facts exaggerated, his speeches contrived …'[59] Shaye Cohen, one of the most authoritative Josephus scholars, concurs, even having in the index for his great work on Josephus entries for 'exaggeration', 'corrupt transmission of names and numbers' and 'inconsistency and sloppiness'.[60] Magen Broshi of the Israel Museum, a stout defender of Josephus, has to concede: 'even if it is accepted that copyists were responsible for not a few of his mistakes … it still cannot be denied that he was by nature somewhat negligent'.[61] It is not surprising that he sometimes made mistakes. His range was vast: he necessarily had to rely on secondary sources of dubious quality.

In dealing with the Quirinius that he does deal with, Josephus was dealing with someone of fair obscurity. There were many such governors and many such provinces. Governors came and went. Edicts were made and more or less acted on. Josephus would not have looked back to the Quirinius passage as a central one in his historigraphical career. There is no reason to suppose that he would have taken particular care over it. It was a footnote to him, added for the sake of completeness. He would no doubt be utterly bemused to see the storm that it caused.

So the possibility that Josephus simply got (a) wrong cannot be dismissed. If he did get it wrong, then Luke walks out with his credibility intact – or at least it cannot be shown that he was wrong about the census.

It is worth noting in passing that there is a great double standard at work here, and in much modern scholarship. The Bible is assumed to be wrong until proved otherwise: all secular sources, however dubious, are assumed to trump all Biblical sources.[62]

Are Luke and Josephus talking about the same rule of the same Quirinius?

Christian apologists often assert, with astonishing confidence, that there was more than one Quirinius, or that if there was only one, that he was governor of Syria more than once. The purpose of this is to make it possible for Quirinius, or *a* Quirinius, to have been governor of Syria during the reign of Herod the Great. This smacks of desperation, and requires some highly imaginative handling of the evidence.

What is the evidence?

Stones and coins that speak
In 1764 in Tivoli, near Rome, a small tombstone fragment was discovered. It can now be seen in the Vatican Museum, and is known as the *Lapis Tiburtinus*. Its date is unknown, but since it refers to Augustus as divine, it must have been set up after Augustus' death in 14 CE. We have no idea whose tombstone it was. The legible words on the fragment are worth quoting in full. None of the lines is complete, but as far as it goes it reads:

'... King brought into the power of ...
... Augustus and the Roman people and Senate ...
... for this honoured with two victory celebrations ...
... obtained the proconsulate of the Province of Asia ...
... again of the deified Augustus Syria and Ph[oenicia] ...'[63]

All that this suggests is that someone who was once Proconsul of Asia was also at some stage involved in some capacity in governing Syria and Phoenicia. It confirms, in other words, that Roman civil servants had a career structure, which is hardly a surprise. It doesn't say that anybody held the governorship of Syria twice, and even if anybody did it doesn't remotely suggest that it was Quirinius.

Then there are the two stones found in 1912 and 1913 outside Pisidian Antioch, which commemorate posts held by one Gaius Julius Caristanius Caesiano. He held the deputy duumvirate of a city: the duumvirate was held by Quirinius. We don't know the date. This indicates, say various commentators, that Quirinius was governor of Syria on an occasion earlier than the one spoken of by Josephus. But it doesn't. You don't have to know much about the organization of Roman administration to know that a duumvirate connotes rule over a city, not a province. To confuse a duumvirate with a provincial governorship is like confusing the Mayor of Nashville with the Governor of Tennessee. But there's more. The city in question wasn't in Syria at all: it was in Galatia. So the confusion is more like confusing the Mayor of Nashville with the Governor of California.

If we're positing an earlier governorship of Syria for Quirinius, are there any vacant slots whose occupants are currently unknown? The only list we have comes from Josephus himself, and indeed there is a space there: he does not know who the governor was from 4 BCE to 1 BCE.

If Quirinius had a first go at the governorship during this period and did a census then, since Herod died in 4 BCE, it would just be possible to reconcile Luke, Matthew and Josephus. There is no positive evidence for this conclusion, and if Quirinius did indeed hold the governorship twice one would expect there to be evidence: it would have been unparalleled in the Roman world, and surely Josephus and others would have commented.

The strangest part of the whole Quirinius story relates to 'microletters' which the late Dr Jerry Vardaman, an archaeologist at the Cobb Institute of Archaeology, Mississippi State University, said that he found on ancient coins and inscriptions.

In his book, *The Case for Christ*,[64] Lee Strobel talks to John McRay, an academic at Wheaton College, and puts to him the crucial discrepancy about Herod dying in 4 BCE and Quirinius not becoming ruler of Syria until 6 CE. But the discrepancy doesn't worry McRay at all. Vardaman, he says 'has found a coin with the name of Quirinius on it in very small writing, or what we call "micrographic" letters. This places him as proconsul of Syria and Cilicia from 11 BCE until after the death of Herod'.[65] He concludes from this that there were 'apparently two Quiriniuses ... The census would have taken place under the reign of the earlier Quirinius. Given the cycle of a census every fourteen years, that would work out quite well'.[66]

Depressingly, the Vardaman hypothesis was regarded by Lee Strobel as the clinching piece of evidence for the reliability of Luke's account, and is enshrined as archaeological orthodoxy in the minds of his millions of readers. It is depressing because the Vardaman evidence is wholly bogus. All Strobel's readers should read Richard Carrier's comprehensive demolition of the hypothesis.[67]

These alleged 'microletters' were less than half a millimetre high. No one has ever explained why anybody would want to inscribe them anywhere, produced the tools that would have been necessary to inscribe them, or explained how they managed to survive the wear and tear of the millennia. But here's the real point: no one else apart from Vardaman has ever been able to see them – let alone transcribe them. Vardaman's work has never been published in a single peer-reviewed journal. And there is still more: it seems that there is no 'Quirinius' coin at all. Vardaman presented a twenty-page lecture on the dating of Quirinius almost a decade after the unpublished paper to which McRay is evidently referring. There is no mention at all of the crucial coin.

This, then, is how the debate has raged. The Christian apologists have had much the worst of the battle, and if there were nothing else to say, one would be forced to conclude that Luke was simply wrong about Quirinius. But there *is* something to say. It involves going back to the Greek and asking an absurdly fundamental question.

What is a 'governor'?

Most of the modern English translators have Luke calling Quirinius the 'governor' of Syria. The translation isn't bad, but it implies a degree of exactitude about the office that simply isn't there. The word Luke uses isn't a noun at all: it is the present active participle of the verb *hegemoneuw*, and would be better rendered 'while [   ] was ruling'. Or leading. Or governing. Luke uses the noun version from the same word to speak about the rule of the Emperor Tiberius, and in the same sentence he uses the verb version to talk about the Emperor's subordinate, Pontius Pilate.[68] The Emperor and his underling most certainly did not occupy the same office. The point is that neither the verb nor the noun connote anything very specific about function or status.[69] This takes the wind out of the sails of those who say that there were no vacant slots for the

Governor's job at the relevant times, and that accordingly Quirinius couldn't have been Governor before the time that Josephus says that he was.

There is a story in Josephus indicating that, with specific reference to the government of Syria, leadership or governorship was loosely described and that more than one person could hold in one place a role so described. He reports that in Syria, during the reign of Herod, there was a hearing before Saturninus and Volumnius, two 'officers of Caesar' (*Kaisaros hegemosi* in the Greek: – *hegemon* – that root again). The details do not matter: the point is that *both* of them were said to be *ton Surias epistatatounton*: both were overseers or presidents or chiefs or governors or leaders of Syria.[70] The bureaucrats in Rome would no doubt have bridled at such sloppy rendering of official categories, but the story opens up the possibility that Quirinius might accurately have been said to have been in some leadership category in Syria, describable with the general root *hegemon,* before he was appointed to whatever office he was in at the time of the census described by Josephus.

There is another relevant fragment of history. The early Church Father Tertullian (c 160–225 CE), who was no cavalier liberal, certainly knew Luke's Gospel, and had a more than respectable knowledge of the Roman world, stated in his apologetic tract *Against Marcion*[71] that the census referred to by Luke was 'taken in Judea by Sentius Saturninus'. We don't know what Tertullian's source was, but it was a source that Luke didn't have or which Luke decided for whatever reason not to use. It seems highly unlikely that, in a tract designed to convince heretics of the truth of scripture, Tertullian would be saying anything which he believed gave the lie to scripture. The obvious conclusion is that both he and his readers would have known that there was no or no necessary contradiction between Luke and the comment about Sentius Saturninus.

One shouldn't rest too much on this: Perhaps Sentius was the man to whom responsibility for the census had been specifically delegated (perhaps by Quirinius), but one would normally say that the census was 'taken' by the overall governor of the province.[72]

Now let's try to reconstruct Quirinius' CV to see if there is anything in it during the lifetime of Herod that might fit. This is where the Antioch stones and the *Lapis Venetus*[73] help. They indicate, without giving dates, that Quirinius was a man who spent at least some of his life doing Middle Eastern Imperial jobs. Between 12 and 6 BCE he commanded the Roman army in its campaign in the Taurus mountains of Cilicia. Ronald Marchant comments that: 'since the only Roman legion based in the whole of Asia belonged to Syria, and since the area to be conquered was contiguous to Syria, it is reasonable to think that Quirinius was placed in command of this Syrian legion and was given responsibility for overseeing the entire region in the effort to pacify the Homonadensians. If this is the path which Quirinius followed, it is possible to see his whole career in the east not simply as a series of isolated events, but as different functions of his overall command of the whole area'.[74] Possible indeed, and actually quite likely. The Romans didn't like to waste expertise so hard won.

Was there another census?

Prominent in the apologists' armoury is the so-called *Lapis Venetus*, or 'Aemilius Secundus'. This is the funerary stone of a Roman officer called Secundus who evidently served under Publius Sulpicius Quirinius when Quirinius was the governor of Syria, and it tells of some of Secundus' (and therefore some of Quirinius') doings.

The stone first entered recent history in Beirut in the second half of the seventeenth century, when it was acquired by some Venetian traders. It is often said to provide definite evidence that there was a census other than the one Josephus writes about. It does no such thing. Since so much has been read into it, it is best to let it speak for itself. It says:

> (Quintus) Aemilius Secundus of the Palatine tribe, in the service of the divine Augustus, under Publius Sulpicius Quirinius the legate of Caesar in Syria, was decorated with [these] honours: Prefect of a cohort from the First August Legion; Prefect of the Second Fleet; also conducted a census by order of Quirinius in the Apamene community of 117,000 citizens; also, when he was sent by Quirinius against the Ituraeans on Mount Lebanon he captured their citadel; and before he was in the army as officer in charge of works he was delegated by the two consuls to run the treasury; and when he was living in a colony he served as Quaestor, Aedile twice, Duumvir twice, and Pontifex. Quintus Aemilius Secundus, son of Quintus, of the Palatine tribe, having passed on, and Aemilia Chia [his] freedwoman, have been laid to rest here. This monument no longer belongs to [his] heirs.[75]

The stone gives no idea of its date, nor of the date of the census it mentions.

What does this do? It merely confirms that there was a census in Syria when Quirinius was 'legate'. There is no reason whatever to suppose that the inscription is talking about a census other than the one we already know about from Josephus.

But this doesn't mean that there wasn't another census. We look below at the evidence about Augustan censuses in general, but in short, Augustus was a man with a mania for enumeration and order. He was the first Emperor and the architect of the Empire's systems. Palestine had effectively been under the Roman thumb since the invasion of Pompey in 63 BCE: it seems improbable that Augustus would have been happy to wait until 6 CE to know exactly what was there, and indeed, as we see below, Roman dissatisfaction with Herod is likely to have prompted a stock-taking exercise before Herod's death.

It is hard to overestimate the poverty of the records from this region at this time. It tends to be assumed that since Palestine was under some sort of Roman control everything was logged in triplicate in a filing cabinet in Rome. It was not so. For most of the time we're guided just by the brilliant but flawed Josephus. There is plenty of room for entirely unknown things to happen.

Luke's opponents accuse the Christians of extrapolating wildly from tiny scraps of data like the *Lapis Venetus* – of expanding the data to fill gaps that can't properly be filled. The accusation is entirely just. But those opponents are guilty of the same offence. They are saying, in effect: 'If it's not in Josephus, it didn't happen.' They are making Josephus' silence a lot more eloquent than it really is.

When it comes to the question of whether there was more than one census, a bit of historical humility is helpful on both sides. On the side of the non-Christians, that humility should involve a readiness to take Luke seriously. Luke's observation that the Luke 2 census was the 'first' one is interesting and significant. He seems to know about at least one other census. Whether Luke had read Josephus or not, he must surely have heard about the great rumpus that the 6 CE census created. A rebellion led by Judas of Galilee was bloodily suppressed. So whichever census he was speaking about in Luke 2, he surely knew about the one in 6 CE. And he thinks that in addition to the 6 CE one there was another. We know of no other from Josephus. The only suggestion that there was more than one comes from Luke. Why should he be disbelieved? And if there was another one in addition to the headline-making one of 6 CE, why should it not have been one *before* then, at a time when Caesar Augustus had indicated to his men out east that he would like to know what his Empire contained? And why should this not have occurred at a time when Quirinius, the old eastern hand who eventually assumed the formal governorship of Syria, was somewhere on his way up the slippery pole of Roman imperial bureaucracy, holding some position of responsibility in the province?

An alternative suggestion: another translation of Luke

Luke 2:2 is generally translated along the lines: 'This was the first registration and was taken while Quirinius was governor of Syria.' But it has been contended that a better version would be: 'This was the first registration and was taken *before* Quirinius was governor of Syria.' If this contention is right, then of course (subject to there being some sort of Imperial decree and some sort of census) the whole problem of reconciling Luke, Matthew and Josephus simply vanishes.

The arguments are fierce, technical and inconclusive. But there is no doubt who has the upper hand. The alternative reading is generally regarded as eccentric and wrong. Luke has to look elsewhere for his defence.

Other alleged improbabilities in Luke

Registration of 'the whole world'?
It is generally assumed that the purpose of such a census was primarily to assist the taxation authorities. Is it likely that there was such a decree, or that if there was, that it spread to Palestine?

First: we know of no such Empire-wide decree from Caesar Augustus,[76] but it is uncontroversial that Augustus embarked on a great reorganization of Roman bureaucracy. We know that this involved a census of property. It was done in Gaul by his stepson Drusus, and such censuses were certainly carried out in some of the wild eastern provinces such as Egypt, Lebanon and Nabatea. It seems likely that whenever it was done and whomever was required to comply with it, the Quirinius census was a sign of the new Augustan broom that swept away the pre-Imperial order. Augustus loved to count things, and boasted how he had counted the Roman nation three times.[77] Unsurprisingly these censuses were bitterly resented, and often resulted in bloodshed. Josephus tells us of Judas of Galilee's rebellion at the 6 CE census, and it is often said that this is yet another indication that there could not have been a census earlier than 6 CE. This hardly follows: straws broke camels' backs even in the ancient world. In Egypt the census went off peacefully.[78]

Second: it is often pointed out that Judea did not become a Roman province until 6 CE. Does it follow from this that any earlier census of the province would only have affected Roman citizens? Not necessarily. The Jews of Palestine were technically the subjects of Herod, himself a client-king of Rome, but no one knows just how independent Herod was. Probably his independence was more technical than real. He held his territory just as long as Rome was happy for him to do so, and so his main agenda was to keep Rome happy.

The observation that there was no direct taxation of non-Roman citizens by Rome is generally true, but it is not quite as simple as that. Tribute was generally exacted from client kingdoms, and for all practical purposes that meant tax. Those taxes of course came from the pockets of the populace. It was for the local potentate to collect them, but the taxes went to Rome just as surely as did the taxes of a card-carrying Roman citizen. The irony is that Roman citizens at various stages enjoyed tax breaks: the non-citizens in the outlying colonies didn't.

As relations between Rome and Herod deteriorated towards the end of the millennium it might well have been that Rome was keen to make sure that it was getting a proper per capita allowance from the province. Occupation was an expensive business, and Augustus would have wanted to see that the Jews were paying appropriately for the benefit of having well-victualled legions in the land. It wasn't all about the money, though. Rome was becoming increasingly paternalistic. Whatever the legal niceties, there was a creeping annexation of Palestine in the late stages of Herod's reign. A Roman-imposed census would have been a useful tool of imperial policy. The Romans knew very well that to name was to control. A census would have told the people and Herod who was really in charge, as well as providing genuinely useful information.

It is also possible that there was indeed some form of direct taxation. Herod had been a pet of the Emperor, earning the titles 'Ally of the Roman People' and 'Friend of Caesar', but he fell out of favour. By 8 BCE he lost his earlier privileges, becoming a mere subject king. We do not know exactly what that meant for Judea, but since such privileges commonly included absolution from taxes, it may be that after 8 BCE Judea was taxed directly. Whatever the case, the cooling of relationships is likely to have had Rome eyeing the imperial future of Palestine with particular care. Rome would have wanted to know what its assets were, and how the territory could best be divided and ruled when Herod moved on or was moved on.

The form of the census

Is it really likely that the census required a man from Nazareth to return to his ancestral home of Bethlehem? What purpose would that achieve? Joseph's link to David was a matter of ancient history. David had died about a thousand years before.

Augustus' success in holding together his vast empire was to a large extent dependent on respect, within limits, of local custom. He urged his regional administrators to be flexible in the ways that they prosecuted Imperial policy. That flexibility might have accommodated an eccentric-looking census in Judaea.

We know little about Jewish systems of property ownership and inheritance in the Second Temple period, but it seems likely that the Biblical patterns of inheritance would have produced a nightmarishly complicated problem for any would-be taxer. The prominence of the genealogies in Matthew and Luke testify to the importance to contemporary Palestinian Jews of the ancient familial relationships. Perhaps Joseph and many others owned tiny fractions of a Bethlehem plot. If they did, it might have made a good deal of sense for all the contenders to be in one place to sort out the fiscal consequences of their ownership.

Christian apologists sometimes rely on an interesting edict of the eparch of Egypt, C. Vibius Maximus. In around 104 CE he issued an order in relation to a census of Egypt. He decreed that everyone away from 'his own place' had to go home for the census. We don't know what 'his own place' meant, but there is no reason to suppose that it meant a return to an ancestral home. It is not a true parallel with the census that Luke talks about, but it does indicate that the census methods used in the Roman Empire were many and various and tailored to the local demands. To that extent only it supports the Christian story.

A much more potent argument is simply that Luke, who would have known about Roman practices, was writing some time in the first century to an audience who would have known too.[79] If what he was saying was ridiculous his absurdity would have been obvious. If the census was a ruse to get Jesus born in Bethlehem rather than Nazareth, the loss of credibility which would have resulted from telling a transparently stupid story about the form of the census would have outweighed massively any theological benefit in having Jesus born in Bethlehem.

Was it credible that the whole family went?

It is sometimes said that even if Joseph had to go to Bethlehem for some arcane reason connected with the first century Jewish inheritance laws, then it is inconceivable that the census takers would have required his pregnant wife to go too. And yes, it does seem unlikely, although we don't know for sure. An edict along those lines would certainly have clogged the roads of Judea. It is much more likely that she didn't have to go, but chose to go.

Just before the birth of my son Tom I had a case in Manchester. It was a very long standing commitment and I couldn't get out of it. My heavily pregnant wife (who is very conveniently called Mary), didn't like the idea of giving birth in London without me being there, and I didn't like it either. So we went to Manchester together, clutching the medical notes in case the baby arrived while we there. Nobody suggested that there was anything strange about that journey. Although I was compelled to go to Manchester, she wasn't. It might well have been like that with the other Mary.

Taking stock: is Luke plainly incredible?

This has been a long and involved chapter, but a few points are clear.

The suggestion that Luke and Matthew differ by about ten years in fixing the date of Jesus' birth doesn't square with what Luke himself says about the time of John the Baptist's birth (which was apparently during the rule of Herod the Great), and the interval between the birth of John the Baptist and Jesus (which was apparently about six months). It also doesn't square with what Luke says about the times when John and Jesus began their respective ministries.

So in relation to the really important matter – the date of Jesus' birth – Matthew and Luke say the same thing.

The remaining question is the accuracy of the comments Luke makes about the date of the census. This is now rather peripheral: he uses the census as one method of fixing the date of Jesus' birth, and we know from the references we've just looked at that he agrees with Matthew about this. The census/Quirinius references matter for two reasons: First, they impinge on Luke's ability as a historian: is he a careful researcher? And second, they relate to Luke's integrity: has he manufactured the census as a device to ensure that Jesus was born in Bethlehem?

There is nothing intrinsically improbable about the idea that the Romans were sufficiently interested in Palestine in the last years of Herod's reign to hold some sort of census. Nor is there anything obviously fanciful about the notion that such a census might involve an inquiry into ancestral Jewish land rights which necessitated a return to a place where one's ancestors lived. As for Mary going there too: well, women like to be with their husbands when they give birth, and vice versa.

But was there, as Luke says, a census in Judea at the time when Quirinius was 'governor' of Syria? The only person who says that Quirinius only became governor of Syria after the death of Herod is Josephus, and he is far from unimpeachable. If Josephus made a mistake about Quirinius' dates there is nothing more to say. But even if Josephus is right, the case against Luke is far from proved.

The key lies in realizing: (a) how vague Luke is in describing Quirinius' position (he does not ascribe a particular rank within the Roman hierarchy, but merely says that he was in a position of some authority at the relevant time); and (b) how vague is our knowledge of just how Rome ruled in its distant provinces. Josephus' tale of Saturninus and Volumnius is a salutary one.

Could there have been more than one census? Indeed there could. The fact that Luke describes his census as the first, when he must have known about the much more notorious census in 4 CE (which is the one Josephus deals with), suggests strongly that there was.

Opponents of Luke's credibility fall into two dangerous errors. The first is to think that Josephus always tells the truth, the whole truth and nothing but the truth. In fact he doesn't, but it is not necessary for the defence of Luke to say that Josephus is mistaken. We need to beware of the double standard that says that any secular source is always to be preferred to any Biblical source. The second is to think that our knowledge of Palestine in the first centuries BCE and CE is seamless: it's not. There are far more holes than there is material.

On the issue of the date of Jesus' birth, Matthew, Luke and Josephus can live quite happily together. On the fact, the nature and the date of the Lucan census, Luke and Josephus can cohabit without any real strain. The strain is generated by commentators, both Christian and secular,

who come at Josephus and Luke desperate to find what
they need to find.

Chapter 4

Born in Bethlehem?

On a chilly winter morning I walked from my lodgings in Jerusalem's Old City up to the ramshackle Arab bus station. I was the only westerner there, and everyone looked at me with surprise. A bus to Bethlehem was leaving in ten minutes, and I got on and ate an orange.

The bus shuddered off, belching, rounded the corner by New Gate, gathered rickety speed as it coasted down past the Jaffa Gate, and then laboured up towards Talpiot.

Jerusalem is difficult to shake off. The stately British Mandatory houses of south Jerusalem soon give way to flinty fields and corrugated iron shacks, but on every strategic hilltop there's a concrete castle with a shopping mall, a children's playground and a lot of firepower. Wilderness is not far beneath these fields. On the ridge towards Bethlehem there's a vertiginous, switchback feel, although you're not particularly high. On the back seat I sweated in a hot wind out of Arabia. The checkpoints were frequent, sullen, cursory and quick.

I had been to Bethlehem many times before, but this was the saddest time. The tourists had abandoned the place, and there was a crushing listlessness. Most of the cheerful tat of Palestine had gone. Usually the olive-wood camels, the crude nativity sets and the winking statues of the Virgin hunt you relentlessly down. Now you had

Central Bethlehem today.

to search for them, or for a plate of hummus and pickles. Even the children selling dusty postcards in Manger Square were tired.

Fields outside Bethlehem.

The entrance of the Church of the Nativity, Bethlehem.
© *www.HolylandPhotos.org*

I bowed to get into the Church of the Nativity. It has a deliberately low door to stop invaders riding their horses in. I have tried long and hard to feel appropriate things about this church, and I've failed. It does nothing for me. I used to think that that was because all the shocking rivalry for control of the church had drained all resonance from it. And perhaps it is hard for prayers to feel effective in a chapel where Greek Orthodox and Syrian monks have fought with mops to the point of bloodshed over who has the right to dust a particular lamp. But I don't think it's that, or just that. I think it is that the miracle which is said to have happened here is too vast to be emotionally accessible.

I went down the steps into the Cave of the Nativity. In the floor of the crypt there is a silver star, and over the star is an inscription: 'Hic de Virgine Maria Jesus

The Grotto of the Nativity, beneath the Church of the Nativity in Bethlehem. The metal star in the lower 'cave' area is said to mark the exact spot of Jesus' birth. © www.HolylandPhotos.org

Christus natus est': 'Here the Virgin Mary gave birth to Jesus Christ.' I stood there for a while, trying again to kick my feelings into shape, watched by a black-robed Greek monk who turned out to be from Adelaide. And then, to my surprise, there was a loud whispering and clattering, and we were joined in the crypt by a small party of Christians with southern US accents. They were hushed by their young Israeli guide, who carried an assault rifle over his shoulder.

They stood in silence, looking at the star, their guide-books, and no doubt at their preconceptions. And then one of them said: 'So this is where it was. This is where the Lord was born.'

'Well, no', said the guide, who clearly wasn't interested in any repeat business. 'This is a cave consecrated to Adonis. Jesus was actually born in Nazareth. You'll be getting the bus there tomorrow.'

The case against Bethlehem

The guide's statement, although profoundly shocking to those American Christians, represents a point of view common in the academic and the not-so-academic literature.

The case against Bethlehem is not difficult to make. We saw most of its strands in Chapter 1.

Eloquent non-mentions

Jesus' birth in Bethlehem is mentioned only in Matthew and Luke, and is not mentioned in several places[80] where one might have expected it to be mentioned.

The evidence of Mark

It is said that Mark thinks that Jesus was born in Nazareth. The evidence for this is said to be:[81]

- There is no mention of anywhere other than Nazareth as the origin of Jesus.
- Mark opens the story of Jesus by saying: 'In those days Jesus came from Nazareth of Galilee ...'[82]
- When Jesus moves to Capernaum, he is universally regarded as a Nazarene.[83] When Jesus returns to Nazareth it is described as his *patris* – his ancestral home.[84]
- When he creates offence by his teaching in the Nazareth synagogue, Jesus says: 'Prophets are not without honour, except in their home town, and among their own kin, and in their own house.'[85]

Bethlehem is a theological device

The literary intentions of Matthew and Luke are quite clear, this argument says. They want Jesus to be born in Bethlehem for purely theological reasons – so that they can say that he is a completely kosher Davidic Messiah. They let the hermeneutical cat out of the bag in their chronologies. Matthew, as he has a tendency to do, over-eggs the theological pudding by his constant (mis) citation of the Hebrew scriptures. This theological motivation on the part of both authors means that they relinquish all claims to historicity.

Other discrepancies between Matthew and Luke

It is said that other discrepancies between Matthew and Luke make it clear that in the whole of the Bethlehem story we are not in the realm of history.

The differences between the accounts are real: they were pointed out in Chapter 1. For present purposes the following elements are particularly significant.

The clear impression that you get from Matthew is that the holy family had always lived in Bethlehem, and that

Mary duly gave birth in her home town. There was no journeying involved. Matthew knows that Jesus had to end up in Nazareth eventually, and so, the sceptics say, concocted the business of the massacre and the dangerous ascent of Archelaus to the throne of Judah in order to uproot the family from Bethlehem and get them, via a very convoluted route, up to Galilee. Luke, on the other hand, has the family as Nazareth residents, tells the census story in order to have Jesus born in Bethlehem, and then, after the usual rituals in the Jerusalem temple, moves them to Nazareth.

These are irreconcilable discrepancies, say the critics. Suppose Matthew is right, and Jesus was being hunted by a paranoid and homicidal Herod. The very last thing that the family would do is to go to Jerusalem, of all places, where Herod lived. It would be putting the neonate's head into the lion's mouth. And suppose Luke is right, and that the family went to Jerusalem and then on to Galilee. Then there is no room at all for a long sojourn in Egypt.

In *Fiddler on the Roof*, Tevye, the peace-loving peasant of Anatevka, is listening to a argument between two villagers about whether or not the village should have more contact with the outside world. 'Of course we should', says one. 'You are right', says Teyve. 'Of course we shouldn't', says another. 'You are right', says Teyve. A third villager pipes up, pointing out that if the first villager is right, the second villager cannot possibly be right too. Tevye listens thoughtfully. 'You know', he says, 'You are also right.'

Christian attempts to read Matthew and Luke together are often portrayed as being as logically unsustainable as poor, well-meaning Teyve's efforts to defuse the tensions of Anatevka. But is it really as bad as that?

The case for Bethlehem

Many of the points have been dealt with already, and where that is so the response is only summarized here.

Two accounts

The discrepancies are real and dramatic. That means that it cannot be argued with a straight face that Matthew and Luke collaborated or had a common source. It was plainly not just one first century account that had the idea of Bethlehem.

'Eloquent non-mentions' and the evidence of Mark

It is notoriously dangerous to conclude anything from silence. It is perfectly true that secular sources say nothing about a birth in Bethlehem, but then they don't say much about Jesus either. It is true, too, that Paul says nothing about it, but that is hardly surprising. For much of his ministry (and particularly for that part of his ministry which is evidenced in his writings), he was trying to make Jesus accessible to the Gentile world. He was trying to play down the Jewishness of Jesus. It would have been tactically silly of him to portray Jesus as the Davidic Messiah the Jews had been waiting for: it would have alienated much of his audience.

The cited non-mentions in the other gospels are perhaps explicable along similar lines. We have dealt already with the various apparent agendas of the other two gospels. Or perhaps the source used by the gospel writer in question simply didn't know the Bethlehem story. Whatever the case, these are hardly reasons to reject two clear positive accounts from two plainly different sources.

Bethlehem as a theological device

For both Matthew and Luke (and very explicitly for Matthew), Bethlehem has a theological point. But proving this is not at all the same thing as proving that the Bethlehem story was made up in order to make that theological point. Simply because things are said to have a wider significance or a particular patently absurd cause doesn't mean that they didn't happen. Take a ridiculous example: Suppose that a cult wrote a polemical tract describing the Battle of the Somme and saying that the carnage was punishment for the sin of a rabbit that lived in Leicestershire. Suppose that in two thousand years time that tract was the only surviving record that made any mention of the Somme. The theology of the tract would be arrant nonsense. But does that mean that the Somme didn't happen? Of course not.

Now take an example closer to the texts we're looking at. Matthew of course has a tendency to theologize – to expound. One of the classic instances is in Matthew 21, where Matthew has Jesus riding into Jerusalem on the back of both a colt and a donkey[86] – a very uncomfortable and improbable ride. He explains that Jesus did this to fulfil a prophecy of Zechariah – that 'your king is coming to you, humble, and mounted on a donkey and on a colt, the foal of a donkey'.[87] Both Mark and Luke, dealing with the same incident, put Jesus simply on a colt.[88] Has Matthew got it wrong? It rather depends on what the question is. If the question is: 'What was physically there to be seen that morning?', Matthew has it wrong. It doesn't seem that there was a donkey as well as a colt, and if there was it is unlikely that Jesus was riding both of them. But if the question is: 'What, in broader terms, was really happening that morning?' Matthew might well be right. Perhaps that prophecy of Zechariah's was being fulfilled on the ride in. The point for present purposes is that nobody looks at Matthew and says: 'That account is plainly written with Zechariah in mind, and so we can conclude that Jesus never rode into Jerusalem at all.'

Did Jesus ride into Jerusalem that morning? Of course he did.

Other discrepancies between Matthew and Luke

One mustn't bend until one's credibility or integrity breaks. Often the response will have to be: We don't know if or how these accounts can be read together. But some observations are possible without doing damaging violence to text, history or common sense.

(a) Matthew doesn't say that Joseph and Mary lived habitually in Bethlehem. He just doesn't talk about a journey to get there. He does indicate that it was their intention, after their trip to Egypt, to go back to Judea,[89] but that doesn't mean that it had always been their family home.

(b) We don't know when the threat from Herod arose. Since Herod killed 'all the children in and around Bethlehem who were two years old or under' – basing his decree on information about the date of Jesus birth that he had got from the magi,[90] it may be that the magis' visit and Herod's knowledge of Jesus' birth didn't occur until very significantly after the birth. If that's so, there would have been no reason to be scared of going to Jerusalem to the Temple in exactly the way described in Luke.

(c) Luke doesn't insist that the family went straight (back) to Nazareth after presenting Jesus in the Temple, although it has to be acknowledged that that is by far the easier reading. He says: 'When they had finished everything required by the law of the Lord, they returned to Galilee, to their own town of Nazareth.'[91] Is there room here for a return from the Temple to Bethlehem, a while there and then, when Herod bares his teeth, a flight to Egypt and a return by a roundabout route to Galilee? Theoretically there is room, but it's not comfortable. There is certainly no room at all for the view that Luke knew about these elements of the Matthew story, thought them credible, but chose not to include them. Their absence can only mean that Luke didn't know about these events, or had heard of them and, after investigation, thought that they were insufficiently attested to be included in his history.

Evidence on the ground[92]

The Church of the Nativity says that Jesus was born in a cave – the cave where the Americans were confronted, perhaps for the very first time, with some hard core scepticism. The church builders weren't parroting that from the Bible: neither Matthew nor Luke say anything about a cave. So where did they get it from? And when did they get it?

The idea that Jesus was born in a cave is a very early one indeed. The Christian apologist Justin Martyr (100–165 CE) says that when Joseph failed to find room at the inn 'he moved into a certain cave near the village, and while they were there Mary brought forth the Christ and placed him in a manger'.[93] [94] It is sometimes suggested that the cave story was a creature of Justin's theological imagination – that he had conjured it to help Jesus fulfil another allegedly Messianic prophecy in Isaiah. '... [his] refuge will be the fortress of rocks ...', says Isaiah.[95] But this is surely nonsense. First of all the reference is only dubiously messianic. Nobody, told that Jesus had been born in a cave, would ever say: 'Ah, then he must be the Messiah. Just read Isaiah.' The link to Isaiah was of no apologetic use at all. And Justin was a very tactically intelligent apologist. Hence the second reason. Justin, as an apologist, would much prefer Jesus not to have been born in a cave, because being born in a cave risked confusing him with the pagan deity Mithra who was said to have issued from of the naked rock and who consequently had cave temples throughout the eastern Mediterranean in the first and second centuries. It was no part of Justin's apologetic strategy to conflate Mithraism with Christianity. Quite the contrary; elsewhere he makes strenuous attempts to avoid it.[96]

Wherever the cave legend came from, it had wide and early currency. The second-century CE author of the *Protoevangelium of James* (which we will meet properly in the next chapter), had also heard of the tradition. Murphy-O'Connor[97] points out that the author is evidently ignorant of Palestinian geography, and so presumably obtained his information about the cave from travellers returning to wherever he was – perhaps Syria or Egypt.

Origen (185–254 CE) notes that pilgrims were shown the cave at Bethlehem 'where [Jesus] was born', and visited himself sometime between 231 and 246. The earliest Armenian version of Matthew 2:9 incorporates the cave legend. Some speculate that this represented the original version which was later amended to avoid too close a similarity to the Mithras legend.[98]

What about that tour guide's reference to Adonis? He was partly right. The cave had been a sanctuary of Adonis. The Church Father Jerome (342–420) lived in Bethlehem, and he notes that 'From Hadrian's time [135 CE] until the reign of Constantine, for about 180 years ... Bethlehem, now ours, and the earth's most sacred spot ... was overshadowed by a grove of Tammuz, which is Adonis, and in the cave where the infant Messiah once cried, the paramour of Venus was bewailed'.[99] But Adonis, as was often the way with Roman deities, borrowed from what was there before – in this case Christianity. Hadrian put Adonis in the cave to annoy the Christians. Adonis was hoping to steal Christian thunder, not vice versa. The Israeli Tourist Authority usually school their guides better than that.

When, in 325 CE, Helena, mother of Constantine and tireless collector of holy places, identified the cave as the site of Jesus' birth, she was basing her identification on a tradition which we know existed in the early second century, and very probably existed a lot earlier than that. Why did it attach to Bethlehem? And why to the cave? One satisfactory, if rather unfashionable, answer is that Jesus was born there.

Chapter 5

Stars, magi and murder: alleged improbabilities in Matthew

This chapter will be brief. We have seen now how Matthew sees his story-telling role, and how he handles the Hebrew scriptures. There is no point in making the same points again.

The critics say that Matthew cannot be believed when he talks about the star, the magi and the massacre of the innocents because:

1. he is on his own in talking about these things – there is no corroboration either from other books in the New Testament or from secular sources;
2. he is dishonestly asserting that they happened in order to convince us that Jesus fulfils the Messianic prophecies of the Old Testament;
3. what he asserts is intrinsically improbable;
4. in the case at least of the star he is borrowing from secular sources that talk about portents in the heavens when, for example, a Roman Emperor is born, and using the comparison to suggest that Jesus ranks at least equal with the Emperors.

On his own?

Yes he is, in each case. But the critics are trying to have their cake and eat it. If Matthew agreed with anyone else, they would criticize him for contaminating them or being contaminated by them. His alone-ness is an indication of a virile nativity tradition entirely independent of that recorded by Luke.

Making stories to fit the prophecies?

We have dealt generally with this theme in Chapter 4.

The star

It is commonly speculated that Matthew is thinking of the weird story of the Mesopotamian magician, Balaam, in the book of Numbers. 'A star shall come out of Jacob', prophesies Balaam, 'and a sceptre shall rise out of Israel.'[100] On the face of it this seems unlikely, if only because Matthew is hardly coy about his linkages with the Old Testament, and this time he doesn't suggest any link himself. Surely if he had wanted his readers to make this obscure connection he would have spelled it out for them, just as he does with many other passages. But if he was thinking of Numbers, so what? Matthew's ability to make connections between a star and a prophecy doesn't extinguish the star.

The magi

Some think that they are all part of the covert Balaam reference. And not just signposts to the reader, indicating that we're in the territory of Numbers, but actually the heirs of Balaam. 'How else could they have recognized the star announcing the birth of the king of the Jews', asks Geza Vermes, 'except from Balaam's prophecy about the Messiah which they had handed down amongst themselves?'[101] He is echoing a much less sceptical commentator, Origen, who records that 'it is said that from Balaam arose the caste and the institution of the magi which had flourished in the East. They had in their possession in writing all that Balaam had prophesied, including [the citation from Numbers 24:17]'.[102]

But, again, the reference, if it is there at all, is hardly a blatant, unmissable reference making a helpfully didactic Messianic point. And if Matthew intended it this way, why didn't he say so?

The murders

This time Matthew does make the connection with an Old Testament prophecy – the 'voice heard in Ramah' – a citation from Jeremiah.[103] It's an odd citation. In its original context it refers to the exile of the northern tribes to Assyria. If Matthew made up the massacre in order to fit with this prophecy it is quite impossible to see why. It serves no obvious theological purpose, he'd have been bound to have been caught out in the lie, and if he was going to be downright dishonest he'd have moved the massacre to Ramah (which would also have diminished his chances of being found out, since Ramah was a much smaller and more obscure place than Bethlehem).

These points haven't been lost on the critics. In trying to impeach Matthew they generally seek to assert that the massacre of the infants is meant to evoke memories of Moses. The little boys were killed in Egypt, but Moses escaped. Jesus, the new Moses, similarly escaped, later to lead his people to the Promised Land just like Moses. But if this was Matthew's intention, why doesn't he say it? Why quote from Jeremiah instead of Exodus? It makes no sense at all. It makes much more sense to say that the massacre happened and that Matthew said to himself: 'That reminds me of that passage in Jeremiah. And Ramah's not all that far from Bethlehem ... '

Intrinsically improbable?

The star

If the star behaved as Matthew says it behaved, then not only is it improbable, but it is miraculous.

Many books have been written, filled with eye-crossing algebra, purporting to solve the mystery of what the Christmas star was. There have been many candidates: Halley's comet appeared in 12–11 BCE. Jupiter (the 'star' of kingship) and Saturn (the 'star' of the Jews) were in conjunction three times in 7 BCE. Josephus tells us about a strange comet and star sometime before the destruction of Jerusalem.[104] But none of these tallies well with Matthew. No known heavenly body could have gone ahead of the magi, leading them to Bethlehem. None could have stopped over the place where a boy was born. And Matthew knew it. He was describing a miracle.

It is not worrying that there are no secular accounts of this. We wouldn't expect them: the accounts we have from the period are terribly sparse.

So if you think that miracles can happen, this might have done. If you don't, then you won't think the subject worth discussing. There will be more on the subject of miracles in general in the next chapter.

The magi

Apart from the star itself, the only thing about the story of the magi that strains credibility is their audience with Herod. Why would Herod have delegated to them the job of finding the infant king? Jesus was only just down the road, and Bethlehem was a tiny place. Surely Herod's police could have found the child easily?

There are too many imponderables for such dogmatic suspicion. As we've already seen, this seems to have been many months at least after the birth, during which time news of Herod's attitude towards an infant rival might have become clear. Possibly, then, the child had been in hiding for a while by the time the magi arrived. The fact that Herod resorted to such a crude tactic as killing all the children in a broad age range in *and around* Bethlehem suggests that his intelligence wasn't very good. It's not surprising. Even modern Israel's sophisticated *Shin Bet* has difficulty finding all the people it wants to find in Bethlehem.

If this is a fiction, it seems an unnecessarily elaborate one. If Matthew simply wanted the allusive resonance of gold, frankincense and myrrh, or to make the Balaam's star point, he didn't need the magi. If he needed the massacre in order to get the holy family to Egypt and then back to Galilee, he certainly didn't need the magi. They just don't serve much of an obvious theological or literary purpose. Matthew just might have put them there because they went to visit the baby Jesus.

The massacre

This is the least problematic area. All scholars agree that a massacre like this would have been wholly in character for Herod. Massacres of entirely innocent people are a dime a dozen in Josephus. Geza Vermes summarizes the consensus: 'Is this story consistent with what we know about Herod's character and volatile temperament? Without any doubt it is. His record of atrocities was a matter of common knowledge in Matthew's time. The list of people whom Herod directly or indirectly put to death is endless ...'[105] Nobody was immune. He was as savage with his family as with strangers whom he saw as a threat. 'It is better to be Herod's pig than Herod's son', said Caesar Augustus.[106] Herod didn't eat pork.

Would there have been other records of this massacre, had it happened? Well, not necessarily, and frankly probably not. Against the backdrop of the day to day brutality of life under Herod, it wasn't much of a story. Although Herod threw a wide net, the numbers of children involved would have been small.

Nonetheless many – and Vermes among them – think that it is legendary; a ruse designed to evoke parallels between the life of Jesus and the life of Moses. This has been dealt with in detail above.

The star: borrowing from secular sources?

Throughout the ancient world the birth or the fall of great men was thought to be announced in the heavens. When Lao-Tze was conceived there was a great comet: when he was born a star plummeted from the sky. Tacitus commented that 'the general belief is that a comet means a change of emperor', so that 'when a brilliant comet ... appeared ... people speculated on Nero's successor as though Nero were already dethroned'.[107] In Jewish tradition it was thought that a new star appeared after the birth of Abraham.[108]

These signs were said to be read by astrologers like the magi. Suetonius tells us how the astrologer Publius Figulus, hearing of the birth of Augustus, cried out: 'The ruler of the world is now born.'

Towards the turn of the millennium there seems to have been a wide expectation in the ancient world that a world ruler would emerge from Judea. Josephus certainly records it:[109] so do Suetonius[110] and Tacitus[111] – although it is not clear if they were relying on Josephus. It would have been expected, too, that the sky would signal such an arrival.

The Christians certainly inherited this understanding of astrological announcement, and applied it specifically to the birth of Jesus. The Church Father Eusebius (c 260–340) wrote:

> In the case of ... remarkable and famous men we know that strange stars have appeared, what some call comets, or meteors, or tails of fire, or similar phenomena that are seen in connection with great or unusual events. But what event could be greater or more important for the whole universe than the spiritual light coming to all men through the saviour's advent, bringing to human souls the gift of holiness and the true knowledge of God? Wherefore the herald star gave the great sign ...[112]

Did Matthew have a similar understanding? Probably. Did he get that understanding from the general astrological milieu of the Near East: of course. But does that mean he manufactured the story of the star so that Jesus would be seen as the one come to fulfil the expectation of a Judean world King, or to make it clear to readers that Jesus was greeted as enthusiastically by the rulers of the heavens as was Augustus? No it doesn't. That would have been a high risk strategy for an author committing an account to papyrus sometime in the first century, in the lifetimes of people capable of contradicting his story about the star.

Conclusion

In a rather patronising passage that accurately summarizes the scholarly consensus on Matthew's nativity account, the authors of the *International Critical Commentary* write:

> Matthew 2:1–12 has the power to fascinate readers and to stay in the memory because it incorporates ever-popular and perennially pleasing characters and motifs: the mysterious magi from the east, the anomalous star co-incident with the

birth of a king, the threat to the life of an infant hero, the warning that comes in a dream. These are things to delight and enchant, to entertain and cause wonder. They are also vehicles of truth when contemplated within their literary context in Matthew … In our view, however, they are not the stuff out of which history is made. Rather do they supplement history as history's addendum …[113]

This view incorporates uncritically a lot of presumptions about how Matthew should be read and about how God intervenes in the world. It allows those presumptions to colour inappropriately the critics' view of what in Matthew can be characterized as history. Matthew is always difficult and often maddening. We can wish that he had kept his expository zeal more in check. We can regret that he used a basically historical field to exercise his theological hobby horses. But there are no compelling reasons to doubt his accuracy or his integrity.

Chapter 6

Born of a virgin?

One late, hot night in Cambridge, a group of undergraduates, having solved the problem of suffering and drafted a reasonable blueprint for the elimination of world poverty, turned finally to religion.

'It's a great shame that the Christians make it all so difficult for non-believers', said Rachel. 'The virgin birth, for instance. I don't see why Christianity needs a virgin birth, for a start, and even if I could understand that, I could never believe that it actually happened. Outside the laboratory and the annals of physiological curiosity, virgins don't give birth. And I don't like the idea of a God who thinks that sex is too dirty to be involved in his entrance into the world. Anyway, isn't he supposed to have invented sex? What's his problem with it?'

'Don't worry', said David, who fancied himself as an iconoclast: 'A lot of the early church didn't believe it either. And it's not surprising: the Bible doesn't teach the virgin birth.'

A necessary belief?

The virgin birth in the early church
In Chapter 1 we reviewed what the Bible, other than Matthew, Luke and Isaiah, said about the virgin birth. And the answer was: nothing.[114]

David had a point about the early church's belief in the virgin birth, although, like most iconoclasts, he overstated things. Since earliest times, most people in the churches have believed in the virgin birth, but some[115] have not. If Mary's virginity at the time of the birth of Jesus were disproved, Christianity wouldn't come crashing down as it would if the bones of Jesus were found. Karl Barth was right:[116] The virgin birth was not a condition of the Incarnation, but an accompanying miracle. All but one of the Apostolic Fathers, writing before the middle of the second century, made no mention of the virginal conception when they discussed Jesus' origins.[117] It seems to have been one of several ways in which Christians tried to understand Jesus' relationship to God. One of the most influential of those other ways was the notion of the pre-existence of Jesus. In the fourth century, Eusebius of Caesarea, no heretic, spelled out the creed of his church: Jesus, he said, was 'begotten from the Father before all ages'.

But the doctrine of the virginal conception gradually ousted the philosophical opposition. It began to be perceived as theologically crucial in the fourth and fifth centuries, as Augustine's notions of original sin were propagated. Sex was seen as the medium of transmission of sin.[118] Most people (at least in the Protestant world) don't see the relationship between sex and sin that way anymore. Many of Rachel's points were theologically spot on. So why believe in the doctrine of the virgin birth? Can't we discard the doctrine now that it has outlived its theological usefulness? The difficulty in doing that is that the Bible insists on the doctrine.

Or does it? Was David right?

The virgin birth in Matthew

Matthew seems clear enough. Mary was indeed a virgin at the time of the conception and the birth of Jesus.[119] He says that before Mary and Joseph 'lived together' she was found to be pregnant.[120] Most scholars accept that this 'living together' refers both to domestic and sexual union. Matthew's citation of the Isaiah passage is obviously intended to say that this was a virginal conception. Matthew's comment that Joseph '... had no marital relations with [Mary] until she had borne a son ...'[121] is saying that Joseph did not have sexual intercourse with his already pregnant wife, but it would be a pointless boast if he was himself responsible for impregnating her. Nonetheless there are those who assert that there is no virginal birth in Matthew. 'I insist that if you come to Matthew 1:18–25 without expecting a virgin birth', says Robert Miller, 'nothing is there to suggest it.'[122] This position seems to me to be utterly unarguable, particularly in the light of Matthew's later reference to the 'virgin' in Isaiah.

Matthew describes a betrothal to Joseph along the usual Jewish pattern. Betrothal generally took place when the girl was about twelve to twelve and a half years old, and at that time a marriage contract was completed which had the effect of transferring the girl from the authority of her father to the authority of her husband. Usually about a year, though, passed before the girl moved away from the parental home to her new matrimonial home. The marriage would be unconsummated during this time, although, since the girl was a wife, she could be widowed or commit adultery in the eyes of the law. If either party wanted to break the marriage contract during his period of non-co-habitation, it could only be done by divorce.

Matthew asserts Mary's virginity, and then purports to prove it by reference to the famous passage in Isaiah 7:14: 'Look, the virgin shall conceive and bear a son, and they shall name him "Emmanuel".' We have already noted that this proof only works if you use, as Matthew does, the Septuagint translation of Isaiah 7:14, which translates the Hebrew *almah* as the Greek *parthenos*. *Parthenos* means virgin, but what about *almah*?

Almah is an unusual word in the Old Testament. It is generally translated along the lines of 'young woman' – *betula* being the unequivocal word for virgin. Why the translators of the Septuagint chose *parthenos* is unclear. While *almah* normally implies virginity, there are instances when it is used of women who do not seem to be biological virgins.[123] Ironically, Isaiah 7:14 is the most obvious one. The reference there seems to be to a wife of King Ahaz.

Parthenos or no *parthenos*, it is hard to see any real reference to the virginal conception and birth of the Messiah in the Isaiah passage. But that strengthens the case for the story of the virgin birth being genuine. It wasn't suggested by scripture. The Old Testament has some extraordinary birth stories, true: post-menopausal women have children;[124] the 'sons of God' (probably angels) seduce the 'daughters of men' and spawn a race of giants.[125] But there is no whisper of a virgin birth. Wherever it came from, it didn't come from the Old Testament.[126]

'In a Jewish context generally, and in biblical usage specifically, the language of divine begetting *never* suggests a virgin birth', says Robert Miller, seeking to dismantle the Christian claim.[127] Quite right. It never does. So if we accept that Matthew is plainly talking about a virgin birth, where on earth does he get it from?

The *International Critical Commentary* on Matthew makes the same point cautiously but well:

> … the Old Testament does not clearly foresee an event like in Matthew. This, along with the lack of pre-Christian evidence for a messianic interpretation of Isaiah 7:14, offers some reason for concluding that reflection on Isaiah's prophecy was not a sufficient cause of belief in the virginal conception of Jesus … If Isaiah 7:14 does not of itself suffice

to explain the Christian story of Jesus' origin, there is no scholarly agreement as to what might.[128]

Indeed there is vocal scholarly disagreement. We will come to it. But first we need to look at Luke.

The virgin birth in Luke

The case for an ordinary biological conception is stronger in Luke than in Matthew, but anyone wanting to make it still has an uphill battle. That hasn't deterred many.

The case goes like this:

At the time of the Annunciation, Mary reminds the angel that she is a virgin.[129] How will she conceive? 'The Holy Spirit will come upon you, and the power of the Most High will overshadow you; therefore the child to be born will be holy; he will be called Son of God.'[130] Luke never asserts that between the Annunciation and the birth of Jesus, Mary and Joseph didn't go to bed. Perhaps, then, God worked in the normal way in the conception of this child. Perhaps when Mary was overshadowed by Joseph, come to claim his conjugal rights, she was really being overshadowed by the Most High, just as the angel foretold.

But it really doesn't read that way. And it's at odds both with the assertion in Luke's genealogy that Joseph was the 'supposed' (not the real) father of Jesus,[131] and with the fact that at the time of Jesus' birth Mary is still referred to as Joseph's betrothed, not his wife.[132] These are both late re-touches, says Vermes; and in the case of the 'betrothed' reference, a 'gauche' one. The late scribal emendation is the very last weapon in the critical armoury, pulled out when all else is lost, and the manuscript still stubbornly refuses to say what you want it to say. In the case of both of these 'emendations', there's no physical evidence of a scribal edit. Vermes is reduced to pointing out that the Old Latin and Sinaitic Syriac versions refer to Mary as Joseph's wife at the time.[133] The fact remains that our oldest and most reliable manuscripts support unhesitatingly the construction that Vermes wishes to avoid.

Vermes opts, fascinatingly and bizarrely, for a reconstruction of Luke based on the 'equivocality of the Jewish concept of virginity'.[134] There are two types of virgin in first century Judaism: a woman who is *virgo intacta* and a woman who has not started menstruating. Thus a girl who has conceived at her first ovulation, without ever menstruating, is a virgin in the second sense, but not in the first. Indeed, in theory, she could carry on having children until the menopause without losing her virginity in the first sense. Applying this notion to Luke's nativity story, the already pregnant Mary may be saying to the angel 'I have not yet started menstruating'. Or perhaps at the time of the Annunciation she was still a virgin in both senses, but ceased, at Joseph's hands, to be a virgin in the *virgo intacta* sense shortly afterwards, and before her first period. This all has the distinctive smell of a commentator trying rather too hard.

The differences between Luke's and Matthew's accounts are sufficiently great to make it clear that they are relating traditions from different sources, yet insufficiently great to call them two different stories. But where did the story come from, and why was it told? We've seen that it's not derived from the Old Testament. What are the other possibilities?

Mere invention to deal with allegations of illegitimacy?

We saw in Chapter 2 that arguably during Jesus' lifetime and certainly after it, it was loudly alleged that he was illegitimate. It has therefore been suggested that Matthew and Luke fabricated the story of the virgin birth to spare Jesus and Mary the stigma of illegitimacy. This is deeply unconvincing. If anyone said to anyone: 'You're illegitimate', and the response was 'No I'm not: I am the Son of God, conceived by the Holy Spirit, and my mother was a virgin', the response would be likely to convince the accuser that his allegation was right. Perhaps that was why, when innuendos were circulated,[135] people who knew the virgin birth story kept quiet. Many of the liberal commentators who peddle this argument also contend, with great learning and enthusiasm, that Matthew and/or Luke doesn't/don't say that Jesus was born of a virgin at all, but that, to the contrary, they are tacitly admitting illegitimacy. The commentators can't have it both ways.

Competition with major figures in the pagan world?

Many major figures in the ancient world were said to have been fathered by gods: the mothers of some of the Pharaohs were impregnated by Amon; Romulus was the son of Mars; Apollo fathered Plato and Augustus, and so on. The ancient world even knew the idea of virginal conception: Alexander the Great is said to have been conceived before his parents' marriage was consummated.

But there is a very significant difference between all these stories and the Bible's story. The pagan stories all involve physical impregnation of a woman by some male element. Usually the god takes the form of a mortal man. Sometimes the penetration is euphemized – for instance when Augustus' mother, Atia, asleep in the Temple of Apollo, is entered by a serpent which causes Augustus' conception. This is a long way from being 'overshadowed by the Holy Spirit'.[136] When the Alexandrian Jewish philosopher Philo (c 20 BCE–50 CE), notes that when

Isaac was conceived, Sarah was alone with God,[137] he's being straightforwardly Hellenistic: he's thinking of the fathering of Dionysus and Pollux by Zeus. He's not dispensing with the requirement for some sort of impregnation.[138] There's not even metaphorical penetration in Matthew or Luke.

What we've got here, then, is something different in nature to anything that the pagan world knew. As a piece of myth-making it came out of nowhere.

Would such an invention have materially helped the embryonic Christian cause? Although such 'my-God's-bigger-than-your-god' type tactics were certainly used later,[139] they were not used at the time that the nativity stories were written down. It would not have worked. No first century audience would think that, because Augustus' mother had been seduced by a god, whereas Mary had conceived entirely sexlessly, Jesus had the edge over Augustus. They would simply have scratched their heads in incomprehension and incredulity. A claim of virgin birth would have generated far more suspicion than kudos. As a piece of Christian PR it would have been foreseeably disastrous. And indeed the doctrine was very dangerously misunderstood and hijacked by those most subtle of Christianity's early opponents, the Gnostics.

The virgin birth and the Gnostics: Perpetual virginity and miraculous delivery

The Gnostics hated the body and hated sex. They saw Jesus as pure spirit. According to them he had no real body. He wouldn't have dirtied himself by being clothed in real flesh.

Dan Brown, of course, has things completely the wrong way round. He tells us that the Gnostic 'gospels', suppressed by the early church, told of a corporeal Jesus who married and had a child. No idea could be more alien to real Gnostic thought. There is no doubt that the early church suppressed the Gnostic writings: but that was not because they said that Jesus was more fleshly than the church wanted him to be, but because the Gnostics were insisting that Jesus had no proper body. The big battle between the mainstream church and the Gnostics was about the nature of Jesus, and it dominated the first three hundred years of church life and thought. There is no reason to suppose that if Jesus had indeed married and had a child, this would have been offensive to the church. But it would have been anathema to the Gnostics.

From the point of view of its early struggle with the Gnostics, the virginal conception and birth of Jesus were problematic. The doctrine seemed to play into the Gnostics' hands. As Rachel, the Cambridge undergraduate, pointed out, it did seem to be at least a vote by God of no confidence in sex. Those early Church Fathers, contending for the church's very life against the Gnostics, must often have wished that Matthew and Luke had skipped the nativity story. They can only have decided to leave the accounts there, despite the great tactical disadvantage they posed, because they thought that the accounts were true.

The danger of the canonical nativity accounts is illustrated by plenty of examples from the second and third centuries – centuries that spawned many Gnostic elaborations of the basic story. Some of these were probably generated by a well-meaning desire to defend Mary against the many allegations of unchastity that were doing the rounds. We have looked at some of them. Others were straightforward manifestos of Gnostic thought – and in particular of the Gnostic distaste for the corporeal. The most interesting of these are the Protoevangelium Jacobi and those books which are wholly or partly derived from it – Pseudo-Matthew, Nativitas Mariae, the History of Joseph and the Arabic gospel of the Infancy.

The Protoevangelium cannot confidently be dated earlier than the closing years of the second century. It purports to be the work of James the Less.

In the Protoevangelium, Mary is not only a virgin when Jesus is born, but remains a virgin for ever. This, of course, is specifically contradicted by Matthew, who tells us not only about Jesus' siblings,[140] but that Joseph '... had no marital relations with [Mary] *until* she had borne a son...',[141] (emphasis added). The Protoevangelium explains away the siblings as the children of Joseph by a former wife, and goes to elaborate lengths to underline Mary's virginity by telling us that as soon as she was taken to Joseph's house, he left to build some houses, and after her marriage she was certified as a virgin by the High Priest.

Every possible sexual contact is made impossible. As a child, the Protoevangelium tells us, Mary was brought up in a company of consecrated virgins. She was brought to the Temple when she was three years old, and lived there, fed by an angel, until the age of twelve.

The marriage of Mary and Joseph is heavily supervised to eliminate any shade of an argument for impropriety. Directed by an angel, the High Priest finds a husband for Mary by assembling all the widowers of Israel. Each brings a staff, which is placed in the Temple. A dove flies out of Joseph's staff, confirming him as the divinely chosen husband. Joseph is reluctant to marry Mary. This is ostentatiously said to be because he has grown-up sons – the point being, of course, that the apparent siblings of Jesus are not biologically related to him. Joseph is warned not to be disobedient, and complies.

If your loathing of the flesh is as great as the Gnostics' was, you wouldn't like God (even if he was conceived in the womb of a mortal woman) to enter the world in the usual messy, bloody way. And so the Protoevangelium cleans up the story. Not only do we have a miraculous conception; we also have a miraculous birth.

When the time is come for Mary to deliver, she takes refuge in a cave, while Joseph goes off to look for a midwife. While he does so, all nature stands supernaturally still to emphasize that the emanation of pure spirit that is about to occur isn't sullied by the stigma of having emerged in ordinary, sordid Time. A midwife is found, and goes to the cave, which is in the heart of a bright cloud. The light fades, and Mary is found there with the child. There is no evidence that she actually gave birth. No blood, no pain, no afterbirth; just a beatific expression and an incorporeal baby.

In the great battle between the mainstream church and the Gnostics, the mainstream church eventually prevailed. But not entirely. It lost the battle against the importation of the doctrines of the Immaculate Conception and perpetual virginity of Mary, which are of course still believed by most of the world's Christians.

Conclusion

The notion of the virginal conception of Jesus was not only theologically unnecessary but, particularly in the light of the early church's tussle with the Gnostics, positively harmful. The church, frankly, would have been tactically better off without it. Its origins cannot be traced to Judaism, and although there are some analogies between Jesus' birth and the birth of some god-spawned heroes in the ancient world, the analogies are not good enough to indicate that the pagan stories caused the Christian stories. Nobody would have read the Christian stories as asserting that the claims of Jesus trumped those of the classical heroes or the Roman Emperors.

Of course the virgin birth can't be proved. But where a claim has no precedent and no obvious benefit, it is legitimate to wonder if it has been made because it is true.

Chapter 7

Born *which* happy morning?

Can we hazard a meaningful guess as to when, in whatever year it was, Jesus was born? Not really. To do so is to pile speculation on speculation.[142] It has recently been suggested, for instance, that the date was September 30. The main part of the reasoning goes like this: John 1:14 says that Jesus came and 'tabernacled' with us. This is a reference to the Jewish Feast of Tabernacles – an impression confirmed by the reference to swaddling clothes (because during the Feast of Tabernacles strips of cloth were used to light the vats of oil in the Court of the Women in the Jerusalem Temple). The magi, says this theory, were Babylonian Jews who, continuing the Feast of Tabernacles tradition, would have stayed out in tents with a hole in the ceiling. It was through this hole that they could see the Messianic star. The shepherds joined them in their vigil – sleeping out with their sheep before the colder winter weather set in.

But where within the Feast of Tabernacles was Jesus born? We're told that Jesus was circumcised on the 'eighth day'. That would be usual for a Jewish boy, of course, but perhaps 'the eighth day' is also the name of a day in the Jewish calendar – *Shemini Atzeret* – which is the day after the seven day Feast of Tabernacles. This fixes Jesus' birth on the first day of the Feast of Tabernacles. Make some assumptions about the year of his birth, and you've got

30 September, 1 BCE.[143] The scholars have not smiled on this suggestion. Most people are content to say that we can't know.

There is no evidence that Christmas was celebrated at all in the first and second centuries.[144] Certainly there was not the same early and passionate interest in the date of Jesus' birth as there was in the date of his death and resurrection. In about 200 CE Clement of Alexandria noted that different Christian groups had suggested various dates as Jesus' birthday: 25 December is not amongst them. The suggestions included 20 May, 20 April and 21 April.

It is not until the fourth century that 25 December is mentioned for the first time. The mention is in a Roman almanac listing the death dates of bishops and martyrs. Throughout that century mentions of 25 December and 6 January (the Christmas date still celebrated in the Armenian Church) proliferate. Eventually 6 January came to be regarded by most of the church as the Feast of the Epiphany – commemorating the arrival of the magi. But the emergence of 25 December can probably be tracked back a bit further. In around 400 CE Augustine of Hippo railed against the Donatists, who stubbornly refused to abandon their celebration of Christmas on 25 December, and refused to celebrate Epiphany on 6 January. The Donatists were notoriously conservative and intransigent. They had emerged during Diocletian's persecution of 312, and had clung stubbornly to the traditions of that time. This is good evidence that from at least the early fourth century, North African Christians, for whatever reason, were celebrating 25 December as Jesus' birthday.

But why alight on 25 December and 6 January?

The usual explanation is that the Christians simply adopted the date from a pagan celebration. There are two main reasons why they might have done this. They might have wanted to make a statement – to say that

Jesus eclipsed the pagan god who was celebrated on that day. Or it might have been a device to make it easier for people to convert from the pagan religion – the idea of evangelism by assimilation: the idea that people would be more willing to embrace Christianity if they would not have to give up the elements from the old faith that really mattered to them.

The modern Christmas certainly contains a lot of borrowed pagan practice. The best example is the Druidic Christmas tree. But it is not certain that the date of Christmas was borrowed.

There is an obvious coincidence in time between the Christian Christmas and many of the winter solstice festivals of the ancient world. That coincidence has led many to suppose that Christianity merely moved into the winter solstice market. The most obvious competitor was the Sol Invictus festival – the festival of the Unconquered Sun – inaugurated in 274 CE by the Roman Emperor Aurelian. It was one of many festivals throughout the ancient world that fell around the winter solstice. For centuries before Sol Invictus the Romans had kept the mid-winter festival of Saturnalia in late December, and every tribe in Europe had a similar sort of celebration at a similar time. It would be thoroughly understandable if the Christians had wanted to jump on the band-wagon of the winter solstice: had wanted to say in calendrical form: 'You worship the Unconquered Sun; we worship the Unconquerable Son, to whom your sun bows.' This might indeed be the explanation for the mid-winter Christmas, but there are some difficulties with the idea.

Until the conversion of Constantine (who died in 337), most Christians seem to have energetically distanced themselves from the faiths of the world around them. It was only with the new confidence given to Christianity by its status as the faith of the Empire that Christians started to adopt (in a way we can trace in the historical record) the strategy of baptizing the old pagan gods and their festivals, rather than rejecting, denouncing and destroying them. This strategy developed slowly, and was probably not much used before the mid-fourth or early fifth century. It was most famously articulated in the letter written in 601 by Pope Gregory the Great to a missionary in Britain, urging him not to level pagan temples, but to consecrate them as churches, and to sanctify pagan festivals by transmuting them into the feast days of Christian saints.

We have to wait until the twelfth century for any mention that Jesus' birthday feast was deliberately superimposed on top of a pagan festival. A Syriac Christian scholar, Dionysius bar-Salibi, notes that in times of old (but how old he doesn't say), the Christmas feast day was moved from January 6 to December 25 because 25 December was the day when pagans celebrated Sol Invictus.

If this is not the explanation, what else is left? There is a curious but very early idea, which saw the conception of Jesus and the death of Jesus as linked in a seamless plan for the salvation of the world. John tells us that Jesus died on the fourteenth of Nisan. In around 200, Tertullian of Carthage noted that in the year that Jesus died the fourteenth of Nisan fell on March 25, which is nine months before December 25. Thus he was crucified and conceived on the same day of the year.

This idea has been repeatedly endorsed by some of the great figures of the church, including Augustine,[145] and is embodied in the dating by the modern Armenian Church of the dates of the Annunciation (when Jesus was conceived), and Christmas. The Armenians celebrate Christmas on 6 January, and correspondingly shift the Annunciation date to 7 April[146] instead of the 25 March used in the Western Church.

None of this really helps us at all in groping towards a historically sound date for the birth. The chances of Jesus having been born on 25 December are probably about 1 in 365.

Chapter 8

Epilogue

If God comes to earth, clothed in flesh, one might expect the story to be a strange one. But we don't. Both Christians and sceptics alike seem to expect the gospels to be told in the flat prose of a provincial newspaper's report of a school fete. And that's how they approach Matthew and Luke. The Christians look briefly at their accounts, see that there are some dreadful difficulties in reading them that way, and run off to bury their heads in the sand and the nativity story in a nursery play. The sceptics read Matthew and Luke, see the difficulties too, appraise them by the standards of that school fete report, and say: 'We told you so: mendacity right at the beginning of Jesus' life story. And it doesn't get any better ... '

Matthew and Luke know that they're dealing with something indescribably big. What we've got from them is their more locally Near Eastern version of John's grand, cosmic opening: 'In the beginning was the Word ... ' They both adopt a strange literary style – a blend of description and exposition. But they tell us that that's what they're doing: they tell us how to read their gospels. Matthew gives us the most explicit lesson, conveniently placed right at the start of his gospel. It is in the genealogy – one of the weirdest and most fecund bits of religious literature ever written. In it he says plainly, by his inescapable misquotations of the Old Testament and his obviously unhistorical and unscriptural enumeration of the generations, that this man, Jesus, is the meaning and the goal of scripture. Nobody emerges from Matthew's genealogy as a verbal inerrantist: nobody emerges from it without a hugely enhanced respect for the essential historicity, authority and depth of scripture.

There is an enormous literature devoted to showing that Matthew and Luke differ crucially from one another on points of history. The classic example is the business of the dating of Jesus' birth, and in particular Luke's attempt to fix it by reference to the famous Quirinius census. Christian apologists, particularly in the Protestant world, have served Matthew and Luke ill. The evidence has often been dangerously misrepresented, to the undisguised glee of the sceptics.

There is no need to bend the evidence. Matthew and Luke can look after themselves. They don't need Roman gravestones, let alone non-existent microletters on non-existent coins. By his dating of the birth and career of John the Baptist, Luke makes it plain in his own book that he more or less agrees with Matthew about Jesus' birth date. That just leaves the census – which by now is pretty peripheral. And as to that, the whole case against Luke depends entirely on the notoriously unreliable Josephus, who is uncritically accepted by the sceptics in just the way that they lambast fundamentalists for doing with the Bible. But in fact there's no need to destroy Josephus in order to believe Luke: Josephus and Luke can live together perfectly happily.

The list of alleged improbabilities in Matthew and Luke looks a lot less intimidating at close quarters. But not all problems evaporate. There remain some significant apparent divergences between the two accounts. The most worrying relates to the holy family's action immediately after the birth. Luke has Jesus being presented at the

Temple on the eighth day and then, apparently, going peacefully back home to Nazareth. Matthew has the family heading off to Egypt to avoid the homicidal Herod. You can play with these stories to try to make them tessellate. Some of the attempted solutions are outlined in this book. But they leave me uneasy. The nature of my unease, though, is very different from the unease I felt before I'd immersed myself in this material. It's an unease with the sufficiency of the suggested solutions to that particular part of the puzzle, not an unease with the integrity of the Bible's account of the story as a whole. On the issue of the immediate aftermath of Jesus' birth, I'm content to say that I don't know. Agnosticism on that issue needn't infect belief in the rest.

As to the virgin birth, of course there can never be any historical proof. Nor, since it is not demonstrably a necessary condition of the truth of the rest of Christianity, can there ever be any theological proof (for those to choose to believe in such proofs). But, despite brave and imaginative attempts to contend that the Bible does not insist on the virgin birth, it is plain that both Matthew and Luke do insist on it. The doctrine was not a device designed to protect Jesus from the stigma of illegitimacy, or his mother from the stigma of unchastity. It was not borrowed from Jewish tradition, pagan religion or a desire to lift Jesus high enough to keep up with the Caesars. There were many profound disadvantages in preaching it in the early church. Perhaps the doctrine arose because it was true.

I will go more happily to the nativity play this year. I will mutter away, as I always do, about the shocking conflation of Matthew, Luke and tradition in the script. But I will say more confidently than I did last year, that the Word became flesh and dwelt among us, full of grace and truth.

Appendix

The text of the nativity stories in Matthew and Luke

(From the New Revised Standard Version)

Matthew

Chapter 1

[1]An account of the genealogy of Jesus the Messiah, the son of David, the son of Abraham.

[2]Abraham was the father of Isaac, and Isaac the father of Jacob, and Jacob the father of Judah and his brothers, [3]and Judah the father of Perez and Zerah by Tamar, and Perez the father of Hezron, and Hezron the father of Aram, [4]and Aram the father of Aminadab, and Aminadab the father of Nahshon, and Nahshon the father of Salmon, [5]and Salmon the father of Boaz by Rahab, and Boaz the father of Obed by Ruth, and Obed the father of Jesse, [6]and Jesse the father of King David.

And David was the father of Solomon by the wife of Uriah, [7]and Solomon the father of Rehoboam, and Rehoboam the father of Abijah, and Abijah the father of Asaph, [8]and Asaph the father of Jehoshaphat, and Jehoshaphat the father of Joram, and Joram the father of Uzziah, [9]and Uzziah the father of Jotham, and Jotham the father of

Ahaz, and Ahaz the father of Hezekiah, [10]and Hezekiah the father of Manasseh, and Manasseh the father of Amos, and Amos the father of Josiah, [11]and Josiah the father of Jechoniah and his brothers, at the time of the deportation to Babylon.

[12]And after the deportation to Babylon: Jechoniah was the father of Salathiel, and Salathiel the father of Zerubbabel, [13]and Zerubbabel the father of Abiud, and Abiud the father of Eliakim, and Eliakim the father of Azor, [14]and Azor the father of Zadok, and Zadok the father of Achim, and Achim the father of Eliud, [15]and Eliud the father of Eleazar, and Eleazar the father of Matthan, and Matthan the father of Jacob, [16]and Jacob the father of Joseph the husband of Mary, of whom Jesus was born, who is called the Messiah.

[17]So all the generations from Abraham to David are fourteen generations; and from David to the deportation to Babylon, fourteen generations; and from the deportation to Babylon to the Messiah, fourteen generations.

[18]Now the birth of Jesus the Messiah took place in this way. When his mother Mary had been engaged to Joseph, but before they lived together, she was found to be with child from the Holy Spirit. [19]Her husband Joseph, being a righteous man and unwilling to expose her to public disgrace, planned to dismiss her quietly. [20]But just when he had resolved to do this, an angel of the Lord appeared to him in a dream and said, 'Joseph, son of David, do not be afraid to take Mary as your wife, for the child conceived in her is from the Holy Spirit. [21]She will bear a son, and you are to name him Jesus, for he will save his people from their sins'. [22]All this took place to fulfil what had been spoken by the Lord through the prophet: [23]'Look, the virgin shall conceive and bear a son, and they

shall name him Emmanuel', which means, 'God is with us.' ²⁴When Joseph awoke from sleep, he did as the angel of the Lord commanded him; he took her as his wife, ²⁵but had no marital relations with her until she had borne a son; and he named him Jesus.

Chapter 2

¹In the time of King Herod, after Jesus was born in Bethlehem of Judea, wise men from the East came to Jerusalem, ²asking, 'Where is the child who has been born king of the Jews? For we observed his star at its rising, and have come to pay him homage.' ³When King Herod heard this, he was frightened, and all Jerusalem with him; ⁴and calling together all the chief priests and scribes of the people, he inquired of them where the Messiah was to be born. ⁵They told him, 'In Bethlehem of Judea; for so it has been written by the prophet:

> ⁶"And you, Bethlehem, in the land of Judah,
> are by no means least among the rulers of Judah;
> for from you shall come a ruler
> who is to shepherd my people Israel."'

⁷Then Herod secretly called for the wise men and learned from them the exact time when the star had appeared. ⁸Then he sent them to Bethlehem, saying, 'Go and search diligently for the child; and when you have found him, bring me word so that I may also go and pay him homage.' ⁹When they had heard the king, they set out; and there, ahead of them, went the star that they had seen at its rising, until it stopped over the place where the child was. ¹⁰When they saw that the star had stopped, they were overwhelmed with joy. ¹¹On entering the house, they saw the child with Mary his mother; and they knelt down and paid him homage. Then, opening their treasure-chests,

they offered him gifts of gold, frankincense, and myrrh. [12]And having been warned in a dream not to return to Herod, they left for their own country by another road.

[13]Now after they had left, an angel of the Lord appeared to Joseph in a dream and said, 'Get up, take the child and his mother, and flee to Egypt, and remain there until I tell you; for Herod is about to search for the child, to destroy him'. [14]Then Joseph got up, took the child and his mother by night, and went to Egypt, [15]and remained there until the death of Herod. This was to fulfil what had been spoken by the Lord through the prophet, 'Out of Egypt I have called my son'.

[16]When Herod saw that he had been tricked by the wise men, he was infuriated, and he sent and killed all the children in and around Bethlehem who were two years old or under, according to the time that he had learned from the wise men. [17]Then was fulfilled what had been spoken through the prophet Jeremiah:

[18]'A voice was heard in Ramah,
wailing and loud lamentation,
Rachel weeping for her children;
she refused to be consoled, because they are no more.'

[19]When Herod died, an angel of the Lord suddenly appeared in a dream to Joseph in Egypt and said, [20]'Get up, take the child and his mother, and go to the land of Israel, for those who were seeking the child's life are dead'. [21]Then Joseph got up, took the child and his mother, and went to the land of Israel. [22]But when he heard that Archelaus was ruling over Judea in place of his father Herod, he was afraid to go there. And after being warned in a dream, he went away to the district of Galilee. [23]There he made his

home in a town called Nazareth, so that what had been spoken through the prophets might be fulfilled, 'He will be called a Nazorean'.

Luke

Chapter 1

¹Since many have undertaken to set down an orderly account of the events that have been fulfilled among us, ²just as they were handed on to us by those who from the beginning were eyewitnesses and servants of the word, ³I too decided, after investigating everything carefully from the very first, to write an orderly account for you, most excellent Theophilus, ⁴so that you may know the truth concerning the things about which you have been instructed.

⁵In the days of King Herod of Judea, there was a priest named Zechariah, who belonged to the priestly order of Abijah. His wife was a descendant of Aaron, and her name was Elizabeth. ⁶Both of them were righteous before God, living blamelessly according to all the commandments and regulations of the Lord. ⁷But they had no children, because Elizabeth was barren, and both were getting on in years.

⁸Once when he was serving as priest before God and his section was on duty, ⁹he was chosen by lot, according to the custom of the priesthood, to enter the sanctuary of the Lord and offer incense. ¹⁰Now at the time of the incense-offering, the whole assembly of the people was praying outside. ¹¹Then there appeared to him an angel of the Lord, standing at the right side of the altar of incense. ¹²When Zechariah saw him, he was terrified; and fear overwhelmed him. ¹³But the angel said to him, 'Do not be

afraid, Zechariah, for your prayer has been heard. Your wife Elizabeth will bear you a son, and you will name him John. ¹⁴You will have joy and gladness, and many will rejoice at his birth, ¹⁵for he will be great in the sight of the Lord. He must never drink wine or strong drink; even before his birth he will be filled with the Holy Spirit. ¹⁶He will turn many of the people of Israel to the Lord their God. ¹⁷With the spirit and power of Elijah he will go before him, to turn the hearts of parents to their children, and the disobedient to the wisdom of the righteous, to make ready a people prepared for the Lord.' ¹⁸Zechariah said to the angel, 'How will I know that this is so? For I am an old man, and my wife is getting on in years.' ¹⁹The angel replied, 'I am Gabriel. I stand in the presence of God, and I have been sent to speak to you and to bring you this good news. ²⁰But now, because you did not believe my words, which will be fulfilled in their time, you will become mute, unable to speak, until the day these things occur.'

²¹Meanwhile, the people were waiting for Zechariah, and wondered at his delay in the sanctuary. ²²When he did come out, he could not speak to them, and they realized that he had seen a vision in the sanctuary. He kept motioning to them and remained unable to speak. ²³When his time of service was ended, he went to his home.

²⁴After those days his wife Elizabeth conceived, and for five months she remained in seclusion. She said, ²⁵'This is what the Lord has done for me when he looked favourably on me and took away the disgrace I have endured among my people.'

²⁶In the sixth month the angel Gabriel was sent by God to a town in Galilee called Nazareth, ²⁷to a virgin engaged to a man whose name was Joseph, of the house of David.

The virgin's name was Mary. [28]And he came to her and said, 'Greetings, favoured one! The Lord is with you.' [29]But she was much perplexed by his words and pondered what sort of greeting this might be. [30]The angel said to her, 'Do not be afraid, Mary, for you have found favour with God. [31]And now, you will conceive in your womb and bear a son, and you will name him Jesus. [32]He will be great, and will be called the Son of the Most High, and the Lord God will give to him the throne of his ancestor David. [33]He will reign over the house of Jacob for ever, and of his kingdom there will be no end.' [34]Mary said to the angel, 'How can this be, since I am a virgin?' [35]The angel said to her, 'The Holy Spirit will come upon you, and the power of the Most High will overshadow you; therefore the child to be born will be holy; he will be called Son of God. [36]And now, your relative Elizabeth in her old age has also conceived a son; and this is the sixth month for her who was said to be barren. [37]For nothing will be impossible with God.' [38]Then Mary said, 'Here am I, the servant of the Lord; let it be with me according to your word.' Then the angel departed from her.

[39]In those days Mary set out and went with haste to a Judean town in the hill country, [40]where she entered the house of Zechariah and greeted Elizabeth. [41]When Elizabeth heard Mary's greeting, the child leapt in her womb. And Elizabeth was filled with the Holy Spirit [42]and exclaimed with a loud cry, 'Blessed are you among women, and blessed is the fruit of your womb. [43]And why has this happened to me, that the mother of my Lord comes to me? [44]For as soon as I heard the sound of your greeting, the child in my womb leapt for joy. [45]And blessed is she who believed that there would be a fulfilment of what was spoken to her by the Lord.'

[46]And Mary said,

My soul magnifies the Lord,

[47]and my spirit rejoices in God my Saviour,

[48]for he has looked with favour on the lowliness of his servant.

Surely, from now on all generations will call me blessed;

[49]for the Mighty One has done great things for me,

and holy is his name.

[50]His mercy is for those who fear him

from generation to generation.

[51]He has shown strength with his arm;

he has scattered the proud in the thoughts of their hearts.

[52]He has brought down the powerful from their thrones,

and lifted up the lowly;

[53]he has filled the hungry with good things,

and sent the rich away empty.

[54]He has helped his servant Israel,

in remembrance of his mercy,

[55]according to the promise he made to our ancestors,

to Abraham and to his descendants for ever.'

[56]And Mary remained with her for about three months and then returned to her home.

[57]Now the time came for Elizabeth to give birth, and she bore a son. [58]Her neighbours and relatives heard that the Lord had shown his great mercy to her, and they rejoiced with her.

[58]On the eighth day they came to circumcise the child, and they were going to name him Zechariah after his father. [60]But his mother said, 'No; he is to be called John.' [61]They said to her, 'None of your relatives has this name.' [62]Then they began motioning to his father to find out what name he wanted to give him. [63]He asked for a writing-tablet and

wrote, 'His name is John.' And all of them were amazed.
⁶⁴Immediately his mouth was opened and his tongue
freed, and he began to speak, praising God. ⁶⁵Fear came
over all their neighbours, and all these things were talked
about throughout the entire hill country of Judea. ⁶⁶All
who heard them pondered them and said, 'What then
will this child become?' For, indeed, the hand of the Lord
was with him.

⁶⁷Then his father Zechariah was filled with the Holy Spirit
and spoke this prophecy:

⁶⁸'Blessed be the Lord God of Israel,
for he has looked favourably on his people and redeemed
   them.
⁶⁹He has raised up a mighty saviour for us
in the house of his servant David,
⁷⁰as he spoke through the mouth of his holy prophets from
   of old,
⁷¹that we would be saved from our enemies and from the
   hand of all who hate us.
⁷²Thus he has shown the mercy promised to our ancestors,
and has remembered his holy covenant,
⁷³the oath that he swore to our ancestor Abraham,
to grant us ⁷⁴that we, being rescued from the hands of our
   enemies,
might serve him without fear, ⁷⁵in holiness and
   righteousness
before him all our days.
⁷⁶And you, child, will be called the prophet of the Most
   High;
for you will go before the Lord to prepare his ways,
⁷⁷to give knowledge of salvation to his people
by the forgiveness of their sins.
⁷⁸By the tender mercy of our God,
the dawn from on high will break upon us,

⁷⁹to give light to those who sit in darkness and in the shadow of death,
to guide our feet into the way of peace.'

⁸⁰The child grew and became strong in spirit, and he was in the wilderness until the day he appeared publicly to Israel.

Chapter 2

¹In those days a decree went out from Emperor Augustus that all the world should be registered. ²This was the first registration and was taken while Quirinius was governor of Syria. ³All went to their own towns to be registered. ⁴Joseph also went from the town of Nazareth in Galilee to Judea, to the city of David called Bethlehem, because he was descended from the house and family of David. ⁵He went to be registered with Mary, to whom he was engaged and who was expecting a child. ⁶While they were there, the time came for her to deliver her child. ⁷And she gave birth to her firstborn son and wrapped him in bands of cloth, and laid him in a manger, because there was no place for them in the inn.

⁸in that region there were shepherds living in the fields, keeping watch over their flock by night. ⁹Then an angel of the Lord stood before them, and the glory of the Lord shone around them, and they were terrified. ¹⁰But the angel said to them, 'Do not be afraid; for see – I am bringing you good news of great joy for all the people: ¹¹to you is born this day in the city of David a Saviour, who is the Messiah, the Lord. ¹²This will be a sign for you: you will find a child wrapped in bands of cloth and lying in a manager.' ¹³And suddenly there was with the angel a multitude of the heavenly host, praising God and saying,

[14]'Glory to God in the highest heaven,
and on earth peace among those whom he favours!'

[15]When the angels had left them and gone into heaven, the shepherds said to one another, 'Let us go now to Bethlehem and see this thing that has taken place, which the Lord has made known to us.' [16]So they went with haste and found Mary and Joseph, and the child lying in the manger. [17]When they saw this, they made known what had been told them about this child; [18]and all who heard it were amazed at what the shepherds told them. [19]But Mary treasured all these words and pondered them in her heart. [20]The shepherds returned, glorifying and praising God for all they had heard and seen, as it had been told them.

[21]After eight days had passed, it was time to circumcise the child; and he was called Jesus, the name given by the angel before he was conceived in the womb.

[22]When the time came for their purification according to the law of Moses, they brought him up to Jerusalem to present him to the Lord [23](as it is written in the law of the Lord, 'Every firstborn male shall be designated as holy to the Lord'), [24]and they offered a sacrifice according to what is stated in the law of the Lord, 'a pair of turtle-doves or two young pigeons.'

[25]Now there was a man in Jerusalem whose name was Simeon; this man was righteous and devout, looking forward to the consolation of Israel, and the Holy Spirit rested on him. [26]It had been revealed to him by the Holy Spirit that he would not see death before he had seen the Lord's Messiah. [27]Guided by the Spirit, Simeon came into the temple; and when the parents brought in the child Jesus, to do for him what was customary under the law, [28]Simeon took him in his arms and praised God, saying,

[29]'Master, now you are dismissing your servant in peace, according to your word;

[30]for my eyes have seen your salvation,

[31]which you have prepared in the presence of all peoples,

[32]a light for revelation to the Gentiles
and for glory to your people Israel.'

[33]And the child's father and mother were amazed at what was being said about him. [34]Then Simeon blessed them and said to his mother Mary, 'This child is destined for the falling and the rising of many in Israel, and to be a sign that will be opposed [35]so that the inner thoughts of many will be revealed – and a sword will pierce your own soul too.'

[36]There was also a prophet, Anna the daughter of Phanuel, of the tribe of Asher. She was of a great age, having lived with her husband for seven years after her marriage, [37]then as a widow to the age of eighty-four. She never left the temple but worshipped there with fasting and prayer night and day. [38]At that moment she came, and began to praise God and to speak about the child to all who were looking for the redemption of Jerusalem.

[39]When they had finished everything required by the law of the Lord, they returned to Galilee, to their own town of Nazareth. [40]The child grew and became strong, filled with wisdom; and the favour of God was upon him.

[41]Now every year his parents went to Jerusalem for the festival of the Passover. [42]And when he was twelve years old, they went up as usual for the festival. [43]When the festival was ended and they started to return, the boy Jesus stayed behind in Jerusalem, but his parents did not

know it. [44]Assuming that he was in the group of travellers, they went a day's journey. Then they started to look for him among their relatives and friends. [45]When they did not find him, they returned to Jerusalem to search for him. [46]After three days they found him in the temple, sitting among the teachers, listening to them and asking them questions. [47]And all who heard him were amazed at his understanding and his answers. [48]When his parents saw him they were astonished; and his mother said to him, 'Child, why have you treated us like this? Look, your father and I have been searching for you in great anxiety.' [49]He said to them, 'Why were you searching for me? Did you not know that I must be in my Father's house?' [50]But they did not understand what he said to them. [51]Then he went down with them and came to Nazareth, and was obedient to them. His mother treasured all these things in her heart.

[52]And Jesus increased in wisdom and in years, and in divine and human favour.

Select Bibliography

The literature on the nativity stories is immense, but there are few books specifically devoted to it. Much of the material is in often inaccessible journals. Where these are important, they appear in the references. Some of the important material – notably Richard Carrier's discourse on the Quirinius census – appears only on the internet. The bibliography below is a very select one indeed. Many of the publications listed include extensive bibliographies themselves. The cornerstone book for any serious scholar is Raymond Brown's epic *The Birth of the Messiah*. The best introduction to the controversies is Geza Vermes, *The Nativity*.

Barrett, J. Edward, 'Can scholars take the virgin birth seriously?' *Bible Review* 4 (1998) 5: 10–15, 29

Broshi, M. 'The credibility of Josephus' *Journal of Jewish Studies: Essays in Honor of Yigal Yadin, 1982*. (Oxford: Centre for Postgraduate Hebrew Studies, 1982)

Brown, Raymond E. *The Birth of the Messiah* (New York: Doubleday, 1993)

Carrier, Richard, 'The date of the nativity in Luke' (2006) Available at www.infidels.org/library/modern/richard_carrier/quirinius.html

Crouch, James E. 'How early Christians viewed the birth of Jesus', *Bible Review* 7 (1991) 5: 34–38

Davies, W.D. and Allison, D.C. *A Critical and Exegetical Commentary on the Gospel According to St Matthew: Vol. 1* (Edinburgh: T&T Clark, 1988)

Gros Louis, Kenneth R.R. 'Different ways of looking at the birth of Jesus: Narrative strategies in New Testament infancy narratives' *Bible Review* 1 (1985) 1: 37, 40

Mason, Steve, 'O little town of ... Nazareth?' *Bible Review* 16 (2000) 1: 30

Miller, Robert J. *Born Divine: The Births of Jesus and Other Sons of God* (Santa Rosa, California: Polebridge Press, 2003)

Mulholland, M. Robert, 'The infancy narratives in Matthew and Luke: of history, theology and literature' *Biblical Archaeology Review* 7 (1981): 02

Murphy-O'Connor, Jerome, 'Bethlehem ... of course' *Bible Review* 16 (2000) 1: 40–45, 50, 54

O'Leary, D.L. *Studies in the Apocryphal Gospels of Christ's Infancy* (London: Robert Sutton, 1912)

Schaberg, Jane, *The Illegitimacy of Jesus* (Sheffield: Sheffield Academic Press, 1995)

Vermes, Geza, *The Nativity: History and Legend* (London: Penguin, 2006)

Notes

1. Perhaps the idea derives from Isaiah 1:3: 'The ox knows its owner, and the donkey its master's crib; but Israel does not know, my people do not understand.' Isaiah is responsible for several other elaborations on the basic Christmas story.

2. Isaiah may be responsible for this too. Isaiah 60:3 says: 'Nations shall come to your light, and kings to the brightness of your dawn ...', and 60:6 continues: '... They shall bring gold and frankincense, and shall proclaim the praise of the Lord ...'

3. John 1:45–46.

4. It is sometimes said that John 1:12–13 indicates John's belief in the virgin birth. This says: '... to all who received him, who believed in his name, he gave power to become children of God, who were born, not of blood or of the will of the flesh or of the will of man, but of God.' The argument goes: Jesus was the Son of God. Children of God are not born naturally. This construction does not square easily with everything else in the New Testament about being 'born again', which seems to be the natural meaning of this passage.

5. Attempts to assert that the term 'begotten' in John 3:16 implies conception other than in the normal biological way have met with almost universal academic obloquy.

6. Note that some of Paul's correspondents seem to be very interested in Jesus' Jewishness: see, for instance, 2 Corinthians 11:5–29; Galatians 1:6–11; 2:11–21; 3:6–21. It is sometimes said that in the light of this interest it is odd

that Paul, if he knew of Jesus' Bethlehem birth and that connection to the Davidic line, never mentioned it. The argument is well put by Steve Mason in 'O little town of … Nazareth?' *Bible Review* 16:1 (2000): 30.

[7] Some at least of the Ebionites, a group of Jewish Christians influential in the early Palestinian church in the first and second centuries, thought that Matthew had misread Isaiah 7:14 (see below), and that Jesus was conceived naturally. But this was very much a minority belief.

[8] Islam also seems to distance God from human sexuality. The Qu'ran asserts that God effected the virginal conception of Jesus in the same way that he summoned Adam into being – simply by commanding: 'Be.' Thus: 'Mary said, "O my Lord, how will I have a son when no man has touched me?" [The angel] said: "Such is the will of God. He creates whom He wills. When He decrees something, He only has to say 'Be', and it is."' 3:47.

[9] Luke 1:1–4.

[10] See, for instance, Luke 9:22; 22:37; 24:7; 26:44.

[11] John 20:31.

[12] John 20:30; 21:25.

[13] John 1:1.

[14] See, for instance, Genesis 5:3–32; 11:10–26; Ruth 4:18–22; 1 Chronicles 1:1–4; 24–28; 2:1–15.

[15] Luke 3:23–24.

[16] Matthew 1:16.

[17] Other suggestions have included: (a) the idea that Matthew lists the descendants of David who actually sat on the throne or would have done so had it continued, and Luke lists the actual biological line of Joseph; and (b) the idea that Luke lists a genealogy that goes through Joseph's father, whereas Matthew outlines Joseph's maternal grandfather's descendants. The reasons for the implausibility of these suggestions are implicit in the criticisms of the other proposed methods of reconciling the two accounts.

[18] Luke 3:23.

[19] See, for example, Vermes, p. 41.

[20] Matthew 1:16 is usually translated along the lines of: '...
Joseph the husband of Mary, of whom Jesus, who is called
the Messiah.' There is, however, an ancient Syriac translation
of the Gospels in which 1:16 reads: 'Joseph, to whom Mary
the virgin was betrothed, fathered Jesus who is called the
Anointed.' Cited in Robert J. Miller, *Born Divine: The Births of
Jesus and Other Sons of God* (Santa Rosa, California: Polebridge
Press, 2003), p. 246. Note, though, that the overwhelming
consensus is that the usual translation is the original one.

[21] Matthew 1:17.

[22] The number 14 is grafted into Matthew's gospel in another
interesting way. Matthew 1:22–23 is the first of a series of
fourteen scriptural quotations designed to illustrate how
Jesus is the fulfilment of Old Testament prophecy.

[23] Genesis 38:13–26.

[24] Joshua 2. Note that Matthew's assertion in 1:5: ('... Salmon
the father of Boaz by Rahab ...') is one obvious indication
that he is not following the Old Testament chronology.
In that chronology about 200 years separate Salmon and
Rahab.

[25] 2 Samuel 11.

[26] See Ruth 1:1–18. Note too Josephus' interest in the idea:
Antiquities 5: 328–31.

[27] Several ancient manuscripts, including the oldest known,
read 'the carpenter, the son of Mary' to 'the son of the
carpenter and Mary.' A few other manuscripts read 'son
of Mary and Joseph'. The overwhelming consensus is that
the simple 'son of Mary' version is the original one. Liberal
commentators such as Robert J. Miller accept the consensus,
and cite the editorial changes simply to indicate that the
innuendo was understood by very early editors. See Miller,
ibid., p. 246.

[28] Celsus: *The True Doctrine*.

[29] Origen: *Against Celsus*: 1: 28, 32.

[30] This appears in several places. An example is *Mishnah*:
Shabbath 104b.

[31] Matthew 1:23.

[32] In *The Messiah*.

33 Matthew 2:5–6.
34 Matthew 2:15.
35 Hosea 11:2.
36 Matthew 2:23.
37 See too Zechariah 3:8 and 6:12.
38 See Numbers 6.
39 Matthew 27:34.
40 Matthew 11:19.
41 John 2.
42 Matthew 26:20, 26–29; Mark 14:17, 22–25; Luke 22:14–23.
43 See Judges 13–16.
44 The Census of Quirinius and the Birth of Jesus of Nazareth. Available online at http://blue.butler.edu/~jfmcgrat/jesus/quirinius.htm.
45 Luke 2:1–5.
46 Matthew 2:16.
47 Matthew 2:22.
48 The Early Church Father Tertullian confuses things further, saying that the birth of Jesus was recorded in the census of Sentius Saturninus, Governor of Syria: *Against Marcion* 4:19.
49 The best summary of these arguments is in a masterly essay by the atheist scholar Richard Carrier: The date of the nativity in Luke (2006): Available online at http://www.infidels.org/library/modern/richard_carrier/quirinius.html. Anyone with any serious interest in the subject should start there. See also Mark Smith, 'Of Jesus and Quirinius' *Catholic Biblical Quarterly*, 62 (2000) 2: 278–93. Smith prefers Luke to Matthew, and despairs of reconciling the two.
50 It is well reviewed by Nikos Kokkinos in *The Herodian Dynasty: Origins, Role in Society and Eclipse* (London: Continuum, 1998), p. 372.
51 Carrier, ibid.
52 Luke 1:5.
53 Luke 1:24.
54 Luke 1:26–38.
55 For an analysis of this possibility, see Smith, ibid., pp. 285–6.

[56] *Antiquities* 18: 93.

[57] Luke 3:1–2.

[58] Luke 3:23.

[59] *Encyclopaedia Britannica*, 15th edition (1997) Vol. 6, p. 624.

[60] S.J.D. Cohen, *Josephus in Galilee and Rome: His Vita and Development as an Historian* (Leiden: Columbia Studies in the Classical Tradition, 1979), p. 276.

[61] M. Broshi, 'The credibility of Josephus' *Journal of Jewish Studies: Essays in Honor of Yigal Yadin, 1982* (Oxford: Centre for Postgraduate Hebrew Studies, 1982).

[62] Probably the best expose of this double standard (in the context of Old Testament scholarship) is in James Hoffmeier's *Ancient Israel in Sinai* (New York: Oxford University Press, 2005), pp. 8–22.

[63] See Richard Carrier, ibid.

[64] Lee Strobel, *The Case for Christ* (Grand Rapids, Michigan: Zondervan, 1998), pp. 101–102.

[65] Ibid., p. 101.

[66] Ibid., p. 102.

[67] Carrier, ibid.

[68] Luke 3:1.

[69] R. Marchant, *The Census of Quirinius: The historicity of Luke 2:1–5* (Hatfield, PA: IBRI, Research Report No. 4, 1980).

[70] *Antiquities* 16: 280 – although there is great variation in the numbering of the various clauses of Josephus. Some versions have it as 16: 9, others as 16: 271.

[71] 4:19.

[72] See C.F. Evans, 'Tertullian's references to Sentius Saturninus and the Lucan Census' *Journal of Theological Studies* 24 (1973).

[73] See below.

[74] Marchant, ibid.

[75] See Richard Carrier, ibid.

[76] The fifth-century historian Orosius says that there was a census in 3 BCE, but he has not been widely followed.

[77] *Res Gestae Divi Augusti* 8.

[78] In Egypt, Augustus instituted a 14-year census cycle.

[79] See, for instance, Lily Ross Taylor, 'Quirinius and the Census of Judaea', *American Journal of Philology*, (1933): 120–33; cited in Carrier, ibid.

[80] Detailed in Chapter 1.

[81] For a good summary, see Mason, ibid.

[82] Mark 1:9.

[83] Mark 1:24; 10:47; 14:17; 16:6.

[84] Mark 6:1.

[85] Mark 6:4.

[86] Matthew 21:1–7.

[87] Zechariah 9:9.

[88] Mark 11:1–10; Luke 19:28–38.

[89] Matthew 2:22.

[90] Matthew 2:16.

[91] Luke 2:39.

[92] The best basic source for this material is Jerome Murphy-O'Connor's stout rejoinder to the Mason article: 'Bethlehem – of course' *Bible Review*, 16 (2000) 1: 40–45, 50, 54.

[93] *Dialogue with Trypho*, 78.

[94] Justin is probably reporting reliably a genuine Bethlehem tradition: he was born in Flavia Neapolis – today's Nablus – just 40 miles to the north of Bethlehem.

[95] Isaiah 33:16: The New RSV translates 'his' as 'their'.

[96] See Murphy-O'Connor, ibid.

[97] Ibid.

[98] See, for example, D.L. O'Leary, *Studies in the Apocryphal Gospels of Christ's Infancy* (London: Robert Sutton, 1912).

[99] *Letter to Paulinus*, 3.

[100] Numbers 24:17.

[101] Vermes, ibid., p. 111.

[102] *Homily in the Book of Numbers* 13:17. Cited by Vermes, p. 111.

[103] Jeremiah 31:15.

[104] The various options are well summarized by Colin Humphreys in *The Star of Bethlehem, Science and Christian Belief*, Vol. 5 (October 1995); 83–101; and by William Bidelman in 'The Bimillenary of Christ's birth: the astronomical evidence' *The Planetarian*, 9 (1991) 20. Available online at

http://www.ips-planetarium.org/planetarian/articles/bimillenary_christ.html.

[105] Ibid.

[106] Macrobius, *Saturnalia* 2:4, 11: Cited in Geza Vermes, ibid., p. 120.

[107] Annals 14:22, cited in W.D. Davies and D.C. Allison, *A Critical and Exegetical Commentary on the Gospel According to St Matthew: Vol. 1* (Edinburgh: T&T Clark, 1988).

[108] *Sefer ha-Yashar*, cited in Davies and Allison, ibid.

[109] *Antiquities* 6: 312.

[110] Vesp. *[Vespasian]* 4.

[111] *Annals* 5: 13.

[112] *Demonstrandum Evangelisum* 9:1, cited Davies and Allison, ibid.

[113] Davies and Allison, ibid., p. 252.

[114] The only references outside the nativity accounts to God fathering Jesus are: Luke 3:21–22; John 1:14, 18 and 3:16, 18; Acts 13:32–33; Hebrews 1:3–5 and 5:5; 1 John 4:9. They do not mention the virgin birth, and indeed they do not mention the circumstances of Jesus' physical birth. Matthew 1:20 is the only New Testament passage that uses the terminology of 'divine begetting' in a context that mentions Jesus' birth: See Miller, ibid., p. 230. Outside the infancy narratives, Mary is named only in Mark 6:3, Matthew 13:55 and Acts 1:14. Joseph is mentioned only in Luke 4:22, John 1:45 and John 6:42.

[115] For example, the Ebionites: see Chapter 1.

[116] See, for instance, *The Faith of the Church* (London: Fontana, 1958), p. 86.

[117] The exception was Ignatius of Antioch. The Apostolic Fathers were those Fathers writing in the age immediately after the New Testament period.

[118] See Chapter 1.

[119] Matthew 1:18–25.

[120] Matthew 1:18.

[121] Matthew 1:25.

[122] Miller, ibid., p. 205.

123 Some commentators would include Song of Songs 6:8 (although the *alamot* there seem to be distinct from the definitely non-virginal queens and concubines) and Proverbs 30:19, where there's a clear sexual allusion (although it is more to the effect that young men have designs on *alamot*).

124 For instance Sarah, Abraham's wife, who was still childless at 90 (Genesis 18:11).

125 Genesis 6:1–14.

126 Beasley-Murray says: 'Isaiah 7:14 was given a greater fulfilment by the Spirit's action than the prophet could have foreseen (that's not unusual for the divine action!).' *Matthew* (London: Scripture Union, 1984), p. 18.

127 Ibid., p. 205.

128 Davies and Allison, ibid., p. 214.

129 Luke 1:34.

130 Luke 1:35.

131 Luke 3:23.

132 Luke 2:5.

133 Vermes, ibid.

134 Ibid., pp. 78–81.

135 See Chapter 2.

136 It has been suggested by Daube that the Passover *Haggadah* regards God as being directly responsible for the conception of Moses, but this has not been accepted by any mainstream scholars.

137 Genesis 21:1. For the Philo reference, see *The Cherubim*, 45. There have been attempts to see Paul's references to Isaac ('born according to the Spirit') and Ishmael ('born according to the flesh') in Galatians 4:29 as indicating a familiarity with Hellenistic ideas of conception caused by the creative power of the Spirit of God. See, for example, James E. Crouch, 'How early Christians viewed the birth of Jesus', *Bible Review* 7 (1991) 5: 34–38.

138 Note too that when Philo comments that when God 'opens Leah's womb' (Genesis 29:31), the Bible says that God is doing what 'normally belongs to the husband' – i.e. impregnation. Philo: *The Cherubim* 46: See also Vermes, ibid., pp. 58–9.

[139] For example, the competition between Isis and Mary: Isis was commonly portrayed with her infant son, the god Horus, on her lap and at her breast. Some of the early Madonna and child iconography was undoubtedly a specific reaction to this. *The Arabic Infancy Gospel*, composed in Syriac, probably in the fifth or sixth century, has Mary performing miracles normally done by Isis. The message is clear.

[140] See, for example, Matthew 13:55.

[141] Matthew 1:25.

[142] The most accessible discussion of the day of the year on which Jesus was born is in Andrew McGowan's article, 'How December 25 became Christmas' *Bible Review* 18 (2002) 6: 46–8, 57–8 on which much of this section is based.

[143] Eddie Chumney, *The Seven Festivals of the Messiah*. Available online at http://www.hebroots.com/heb_roots.html#sevenfestivalsbook.

[144] There is no mention, for instance, in the works of Irenaeus (c 130–200) or Tertullian (c 160–225). Indeed Origen of Alexandria (c 165–264) mocks Roman birthday festivities as contemptible pagan practises – perhaps a positive indication that the Christians did not celebrate the birth of Jesus.

[145] In *On the Trinity* (c 399–419).

[146] Curiously not 6 April.

Index